# THE
# PLATINUM
# QUEEN

# THE
# PLATINUM
# QUEEN

## Over 75 Speeches Given by Britain's
## Longest-Reigning Monarch

Foreword by Jennie Bond
Additional text by Derek Wyatt

The Queen poses for a Silver Jubilee portrait in the Throne Room of
Buckingham Palace in February 1977.

The Queen and Duke of Edinburgh on the estate at Balmoral Castle, Scotland, during the Royal Family's annual holiday in August 1972. The image was also used on an Australian post office stamp to commemorate the Silver Jubilee in 1977.

# CONTENTS

FOREWORD by Jennie Bond
INTRODUCTIONS AND AFTERWORD by Derek Wyatt

# FOREWORD

## *A Christmas Tradition*

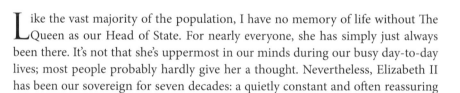

Like the vast majority of the population, I have no memory of life without The Queen as our Head of State. For nearly everyone, she has simply just always been there. It's not that she's uppermost in our minds during our busy day-to-day lives; most people probably hardly give her a thought. Nevertheless, Elizabeth II has been our sovereign for seven decades: a quietly constant and often reassuring presence in the fabric of our national life.

She is certainly one of the most famous women in the world, and yet only a handful of people can claim to know The Queen's true character. She is an enigma, and that's exactly how she likes it. After all, constitutional monarchs are expected to be neutral in all matters, rigidly apolitical and to keep any privately held opinions strictly to themselves.

But The Queen's annual Christmas message is one of those rare occasions when she speaks personally, instead of on behalf of the Government. And, over the years, her words and chosen themes have provided some insight into what really matters to her.

Her deeply held Christian faith and values always shine through. Her responsibility towards the armed services personnel, many of whom have to spend Christmas away from their families, is something she takes extremely seriously. Her commitment to the Commonwealth is another frequent theme and, although she's not a woman given to public displays of emotion, her compassion for those who have suffered loss or devastation is clear. As she's grown older, she has forged more of a connection with people dealing with grief by talking about her own feelings of loss – over the death of her sister, her mother and her husband.

One characteristic that sadly doesn't seem to make it into her Christmas message is her sense of fun. Elizabeth has a wry, dry humour and enjoys making impromptu one-liners: for example telling world leaders at the G7 summit in Cornwall in 2021 to cheer up for a photo. 'Are you meant to look as if you're enjoying yourselves?' she joked.

At another summit thirty years earlier, she was caught on film talking to the (then) US Secretary of State, James Baker, and Britain's former Prime Minister Edward Heath, about the difficulties of confronting Saddam Hussein face to face in Iraq. Mr Heath boasted that he'd managed to go to Baghdad, even if Mr Baker hadn't. Heath's remark brought a peal of laughter from The Queen. 'I know you did,' she chortled, putting her hand on the ex-PM's arm, 'But you're expendable now.'

My own experience of The Queen after more than thirty years of reporting on the royal family is of an essentially shy woman who was plunged into one of the most public roles on earth. If her uncle, King Edward VIII, hadn't abdicated, her destiny would have been very different. She could have led a relatively quiet life, indulging her passion for horses, dogs and the countryside, with the odd royal engagement thrown in to show willing.

But all that changed when she was ten years old and her father suddenly became King. It was from her parents, who had this unwelcome role thrust upon them, that Elizabeth learned the concept of duty. And that good, old-fashioned concept has guided her throughout her reign. She publicly committed herself to a life of service in a landmark speech when she was twenty-one, and she has repeated that vow at subsequent milestones. It is her firm belief that it is her God-given duty to serve as Queen until the end of her days.

Over the years, duty has often had to take precedence over motherhood. When she came to the throne, she was a young mother with two children under the age of four. And, despite the luxury of nannies and servants, she must have felt the same guilt that all working mothers recognise. Not that many of us are called away on foreign tours, often around many Commonwealth countries in one go, for up to five months at a time. Elizabeth was about as far removed from a hands-on mother as it's possible to be.

But in her view, that's just how it had to be. Did it harm her relationship with her children? Probably. Do they resent her for it? Almost certainly not. As they've grown up and taken on their own royal duties, all four of her children have understood the demands put upon their mother and remained loyal and loving towards her. And they wouldn't accept the view that she is emotionally somewhat of a cold fish. As HRH Prince Charles once put it, his mother was 'not indifferent so much as detached'.

She certainly wasn't a cold fish with the love of her life: her husband of more than seventy years, HRH Prince Philip. She was knocked out by his good looks when she was just thirteen, and that attraction never faded. The young Princess was a stunning woman, with a figure to match. Something the Duke appreciated.

One of his close friends once commented that the Prince had a capacity for love that had been waiting to be unlocked when he met Elizabeth. She had unlocked it and, as a couple, they were 'very cosy, very giggly'. And when this same person remarked that they'd only just realised what a marvellous complexion Elizabeth had, Prince Philip laughed and said: 'Yes, and she's like that all over!'

I discovered for myself that The Queen is not averse to a compliment when I met her at Windsor Castle just after visiting an exhibition of royal wedding dresses. I'd been astonished by the minuscule waist on the gown she wore at her wedding in 1947: she certainly was a slender, busty bride. So I told her so, and she let out a little giggle with a dazzling smile.

Wife, mother, grandmother, great-grandmother, Sovereign, and Chief Executive of 'The Firm', The Queen has faced a daunting task over the past seventy years. There has been turmoil in the country and turmoil in her family. But at the end of each of those years, bar one, she has checked in with us, offering her Yuletide greetings along with some words of comfort and hope, born of a lifetime of experience – and the wisdom that begets.

JENNIE BOND

The Queen and The Duke of Edinburgh on their wedding day, 20 November 1947. The ceremony at Westminster Abbey was broadcast live on radio to forty-two countries.

*Top:* Prime Minister Winston Churchill joins the Royal Family on the balcony of Buckingham Palace for a victory wave during VE day celebrations in 1945; *Above:* At her own insistence, Princess Elizabeth joined the A.T.S (Auxiliary Territorial Service) in 1945, training to drive and maintain ambulances; *Opposite:* King George VI and Queen Elizabeth with their daughters Princesses Elizabeth and Margaret (front) at Windsor in April 1940.

# 1952 ~ 1961

*The Second*
# ELIZABETHAN AGE

The glamorous young monarch attends the royal premiere
of a film in Leicester Square, 1952.

Elizabeth II instigated the Second Elizabethan Age. This stands as an extraordinary achievement. Before she was ten, Princess Elizabeth must have thought she was destined for a different, quieter time, as a royal once removed from the limelight. But Edward VIII, her uncle, abdicated from the throne on 10 December 1936, and her life was changed forever. Her father, Prince Albert, Duke of York and Edward's younger brother, was suddenly upgraded to become the new king: King George VI. He was king of the United Kingdom and the British Commonwealth and concurrently Emperor of India (no less). Prince Albert, a gentle man who found public speaking a challenge, assumed office on 11 December 1936 and died on 6 February 1952.

Elizabeth was away overseas on a tour of East Africa, Australia and New Zealand when she heard the news. She had been staying at Treetops hotel in Kenya, and visiting Sagana, a fishing lodge in the foothills of Mount Kenya that was a wedding present from Kenya, then a British colony. Parliament was adjourned, some television programmes were taken off the air, and cinemas, sports grounds and theatres were closed. It was a profound shock to the nation. Notwithstanding, by evening, Princess Elizabeth, now back home in the UK, had become Queen Elizabeth II: it was as if 'the show must go on'.

In some ways the 1950s and the first few years of the 1960s will be remembered most for what happened in 1953, the year of Elizabeth II's coronation. It was an extraordinary year. There were the North Sea floods killing hundreds – even sinking a submarine at the naval dockyard at Sheerness, whilst in Aldeburgh, boats were seen being rowed up the former high street. The floods were devastating and many of the current sea-defences visible today are their legacy, which were severely tested again in the floods of early 1978. In sport, there was much to celebrate. Blackpool beat Bolton Wanderers at Wembley in a seven-goal thriller to win the FA Cup 4-3, having earlier been down 1-3. The legendary Stanley Matthews, a mere stripling at thirty eight, had had a field day. In the summer, Len Hutton captained England to an Ashes home win. The exceptional mountaineers, Sherpa Tensing Norgay and Kiwi Edmund Hillary, conquered Mount Everest for the very first time. At his twenty-eighth attempt, Gordon Richards won the Derby. He was summoned from the winners' enclosure to be congratulated by The Queen. Oh,

to have been there. And to think he had only been champion jockey twenty-six times. No wonder he was knighted. It was not all good news. England disappointed at Wembley and were thrashed 6-3 by Hungary. Many critics thought this was the end of football as we knew it. Some still hold that view today. What a pity medical student and amateur athlete Roger Bannister could not bring himself to break the four-minute mile to crown a great year, but a year later he did so at the Iffley Road track at Oxford University. He became a respected neurologist, and a memorial stone to Sir Roger Bannister CH CBE was unveiled in the Scientists' Corner in Westminster Abbey on 28 September 2021, alongside Sir Isaac Newton, Charles Darwin and Professor Stephen Hawking.

There were other highlights too. Ian Fleming published his first James Bond novel, *Casino Royale*, launching a series that continues to this day, the baton having been passed to other writers since Fleming's death in 1964. *No Time to Die*, released in cinemas worldwide in October 2021, was the twenty-fifth Bond film. Two programmes that have stood the test of time started on the BBC : *Watch with Mother* (which seems just a tad twee when viewed from 2022) and *Panorama*. The brilliant duo of James Watson and Francis Crick discovered the structure of the DNA molecule and changed our lives forever. They were to win the Nobel Prize in 1962. But their fellow scientist Rosalind Franklin, who first obtained the images of DNA that enabled their discovery, was not similarly acknowledged. It was a truly shocking omission. And in music it was hard to escape Elvis Presley, Chuck Berry, Ray Charles, Frank Sinatra and of course, the legendary composer and performer Sam Cooke. Jazz too, took a hold with the opening of Ronnie Scott's in Soho in 1959, which remains arguably the greatest jazz club in the world. Miles Davis, Ella Fitzgerald, Charlie Parker, Art Tatum and Nina Simone regularly performed there. Meanwhile, Woody Guthrie and Pete Seeger introduced us to an earthy style of folk music.

New words, new inventions and new fads also took hold in this decade, highlights including: rock and roll; Sputnik (the first artificial Earth satellite); yo-yos; 3-D spectacles; Bebop; I-Spy books; hoola-hoops; ITV; *The Goons* (a British radio comedy programme); *Private Eye* (a new satirical and current affairs magazine); mini (the skirt) Mini (the car); the first hovercraft; the modem; the M1 motorway; Monty Python; *Hancock's Half Hour;* non-stick pans; Velcro, *The Frost Report;* the Eurovision Song Contest and the black box.

Politics was dominated by the Suez Crisis in 1956, which saw the obsessive prime minister Anthony Eden (who thought President Nasser of Egypt to be a modern version of fascist former prime minister of Italy, Benito Mussolini) replaced by Harold Macmillan. Known as 'Super Mac', the prime minister gave one of the great speeches of his life in Cape Town in 1960, prophesying that a

'wind of change' was blowing through the African continent. The Tories held Parliament throughout with wins in 1951, 1955 and 1959. In America, the young JFK won the 1960 Presidential election against 'tricky-dicky' Nixon.

Of all that happened during the 1950s, though, perhaps the era will be best remembered for the coronation of Elizabeth II at Westminster Abbey. The ceremony was broadcast live on the BBC – a first – though the Archbishop of Canterbury, Sir Winston Churchill and the whole Cabinet opposed it! Thankfully, viewers at the time didn't notice Elizabeth's pause on the way to the throne when her robes got caught in the gold and blue carpet that lined the Abbey's medieval floor, which seemed to have been laid the wrong way. As The Queen said in a recent BBC interview: 'At one moment, I was going against the pile of the carpet and I couldn't move at all. They hadn't thought of that.'

# 1952

*After her Accession on 6 February 1952, The Queen made her first Christmas Broadcast live on the radio from her study at Sandringham, Norfolk. In her message, she paid tribute to her late father, and asked people to remember her at the time of her Coronation the following June.*

Each Christmas, at this time, my beloved father broadcast a message to his people in all parts of the world. Today I am doing this to you, who are now my people. As he used to do, I am speaking to you from my own home, where I am spending Christmas with my family; and let me say at once how I hope that your children are enjoying themselves as much as mine are on a day which is especially the children's festival, kept in honour of the Child born at Bethlehem nearly two thousand years ago. Most of you to whom I am speaking will be in your own homes, but I have a special thought for those who are serving their country in distant lands far from their families. Wherever you are, either at home or away, in snow or in sunshine, I give you my affectionate greetings, with every good wish for Christmas and the New Year.

At Christmas our thoughts are always full of our homes and our families. This is the day when members of the same family try to come together, or if separated by distance or events meet in spirit and affection by exchanging greetings. But we belong, you and I, to a far larger family. We belong, all of us, to the British Commonwealth and Empire, that immense union of nations, with their homes set in all the four corners of the earth. Like our own families, it can be a great power for good — a force which I believe can be of immeasurable benefit to all humanity.

My father, and my grandfather before him, worked all their lives to unite our peoples ever more closely, and to maintain its ideals which were so near to their hearts. I shall strive to carry on their work. Already you have given me strength to do so. For, since my accession ten months ago, your loyalty and affection have been an immense support and encouragement. I want to take this Christmas Day, my first opportunity, to thank you with all my heart.

Many grave problems and difficulties confront us all, but with a new faith in the old and splendid beliefs given us by our forefathers, and the strength to venture beyond the safeties of the past, I know we shall be worthy of our duty. Above all, we must keep alive that courageous spirit of adventure that is the finest quality of youth; and

by youth I do not just mean those who are young in years; I mean too all those who are young in heart, no matter how old they may be. That spirit still flourishes in this old country and in all the younger countries of our Commonwealth. On this broad foundation let us set out to build a truer knowledge of ourselves and our fellowmen, to work for tolerance and understanding among the nations and to use the tremendous forces of science and learning for the betterment of man's lot upon this earth. If we can do these three things with courage, with generosity and with humility, then surely we shall achieve that 'Peace on earth, Goodwill toward men' which is the eternal message of Christmas, and the desire of us all.

At my Coronation next June, I shall dedicate myself anew to your service. I shall do so in the presence of a great congregation, drawn from every part of the Commonwealth and Empire, while millions outside Westminster Abbey will hear the promises and the prayers being offered up within its walls, and see much of the ancient ceremony in which Kings and Queens before me have taken part through century upon century. You will be keeping it as a holiday; but I want to ask you all, whatever your religion may be, to pray for me on that day – to pray that God may give me wisdom and strength to carry out the solemn promises I shall be making, and that I may faithfully serve Him and you, all the days of my life.

May God bless and guide you all through the coming year.

The Queen makes her first ever Christmas Broadcast from the library at Sandringham House, Norfolk on 25 December.

# 2 JUNE 1953
# THE CORONATION

*Following her coronation on 2 June 1953, The Queen made a broadcast in the evening,*
*reflecting on the events of the day, thanking the public for their support and*
*promising to serve the nation.*

When I spoke to you last, at Christmas, I asked you all, whatever your religion, to pray for me on the day of my Coronation – to pray that God would give me wisdom and strength to carry out the promises that I should then be making.

Throughout this memorable day I have been uplifted and sustained by the knowledge that your thoughts and prayers were with me. I have been aware all the time that my peoples, spread far and wide throughout every continent and ocean in the world, were united to support me in the task to which I have now been dedicated with such solemnity. Many thousands of you came to London from all parts of the Commonwealth and Empire to join in the ceremony, but I have been conscious too of the millions of others who have shared in it by means of wireless or television in their homes. All of you, near or far, have been united in one purpose. It is hard for me to find words in which to tell you of the strength that this knowledge has given me.

The ceremonies you have seen today are ancient, and some of their origins are veiled in the mists of the past. But their spirit and their meaning shine through the ages never, perhaps, more brightly than now. I have in sincerity pledged myself to your service, as so many of you are pledged to mine. Throughout all my life and with all my heart I shall strive to be worthy of your trust.

In this resolve I have my husband to support me. He shares all my ideals and all my affection for you. Then, although my experience is so short and my task so new, I have in my parents and grandparents an example which I can follow with certainty and with confidence.

There is also this. I have behind me not only the splendid traditions and the annals of more than a thousand years but the living strength and majesty of the Commonwealth and Empire; of societies old and new; of lands and races different in history and origins but all, by God's Will, united in spirit and in aim.

Therefore I am sure that this, my Coronation, is not the symbol of a power and a splendour that are gone but a declaration of our hopes for the future, and for the years I may, by God's Grace and Mercy, be given to reign and serve you as your Queen.

I have been speaking of the vast regions and varied peoples to whom I owe my duty but there has also sprung from our island home a theme of social and political thought which constitutes our message to the world and through the changing generations has found acceptance both within and far beyond my Realms.

Parliamentary institutions, with their free speech and respect for the rights of minorities, and the inspiration of a broad tolerance in thought and expression – all this we conceive to be a precious part of our way of life and outlook.

During recent centuries, this message has been sustained and invigorated by the immense contribution, in language, literature, and action, of the nations of our Commonwealth overseas. It gives expression, as I pray it always will, to living principles, as sacred to the Crown and Monarchy as to its many Parliaments and Peoples. I ask you now to cherish them – and practise them too; then we can go forward together in peace, seeking justice and freedom for all men.

As this day draws to its close, I know that my abiding memory of it will be, not only the solemnity and beauty of the ceremony, but the inspiration of your loyalty and affection. I thank you all from a full heart. God bless you all.

*Overleaf,* scenes from Coronation Day. *Above:* The Queen is crowned with St Edward's Crown (made in 1661) and holds two sceptres. At the end of the ceremony her crown is exchanged for the Imperial State Crown, which is the crown she wears at the State Opening of Parliament;
*below:* The newly crowned Queen Elizabeth II travels back to Buckingham Palace in the Gold State Coach;

*above:* The Queen, now wearing the Imperial State Crown, and The Duke of Edinburgh wave to the crowds from Buckingham Palace;
*below;* although they didn't come to Westminster Abbey, a young Prince Charles and Princess Anne joined their parents and grandmother (far right) on the Buckingham Palace balcony.

# 1953

*At the end of 1953 The Queen and The Duke of Edinburgh were at the start of a six-month tour of the Commonwealth on the Royal Yacht* Britannia. *On Christmas Day, they were in Auckland, New Zealand, where The Queen recorded her Christmas Broadcast for the radio at Government House.*

Last Christmas I spoke to you from England; this year I am doing so from New Zealand. Auckland, which I reached only two days ago, is, I suppose, as far as any city in the world from London, and I have travelled some thousands of miles through many changing scenes and climates on my voyage here. Despite all that, however, I find myself today completely and most happily at home. Of course, we all want our children at Christmas time — for that is the season above all others when each family gathers at its own hearth. I hope that perhaps mine are listening to me now and I am sure that when the time comes they, too, will be great travellers.

My husband and I left London a month ago, but we have already paid short visits to Bermuda, Jamaica, Fiji and Tonga, and have passed through Panama. I should like to thank all our hosts very warmly for the kindness of their welcome and the great pleasure of our stay. In a short time we shall be visiting Australia and later Ceylon and before we end this great journey we shall catch a glimpse of other places in Asia, Africa and in the Mediterranean.

So this will be a voyage right round the world — the first that a Queen of England has been privileged to make as Queen. But what is really important to me is that I set out on this journey in order to see as much as possible of the people and countries of the Commonwealth and Empire, to learn at first hand something of their triumphs and difficulties and something of their hopes and fears.

At the same time I want to show that the Crown is not merely an abstract symbol of our unity but a personal and living bond between you and me. Some people have expressed the hope that my reign may mark a new Elizabethan age. Frankly I do not myself feel at all like my great Tudor forbear, who was blessed with neither husband nor children, who ruled as a despot and was never able to leave her native shores.

But there is at least one very significant resemblance between her age and mine. For her Kingdom, small though it may have been and poor by comparison with her European neighbours, was yet great in spirit and well endowed with men who were ready to encompass the earth. Now, this great Commonwealth, of which I am

From late 1953 to mid 1954, the Royal couple toured the Commonwealth Nations.
Here The Queen, looking cool and chic in her New Look style dress and peep-toe
sandals, leaves the House of Assembly, Bermuda with Prince Philip.

*I set out on this journey in order to see as much as possible of the people and countries of the Commonwealth and Empire, to learn at first hand something of their triumphs and difficulties and something of their hopes and fears.*

so proud to be the Head, and of which that ancient Kingdom forms a part, though rich in material resources is richer still in the enterprise and courage of its peoples.

Little did those adventurous heroes of Tudor and Stuart times realise what would grow from the settlements which they and later pioneers founded. From the Empire of which they built the frame, there has arisen a world-wide fellowship of nations of a type never seen before. In that fellowship the United Kingdom is an equal partner with many other proud and independent nations, and she is leading yet other still backward territories forward to the same goal. All these nations have helped to create our Commonwealth, and all are equally concerned to maintain, develop and defend it against any challenge that may come.

As I travel across the world today I am ever more deeply impressed with the achievement and the opportunity which the modern Commonwealth presents. Like New Zealand, from whose North Island I am speaking, every one of its nations can be justly proud of what it has built for itself on its own soil. But their greatest achievement, I suggest, is the Commonwealth itself, and that owes much to all of them. Thus formed, the Commonwealth bears no resemblance to the Empires of the past. It is an entirely new conception, built on the highest qualities of the spirit of man: friendship, loyalty and the desire for freedom and peace. To that new conception of an equal partnership of nations and races I shall give myself heart and soul every day of my life. I wished to speak of it from New Zealand this Christmas Day because we are celebrating the birth of the Prince of Peace, who preached the brotherhood of man. May that brotherhood be furthered by all our thoughts and deeds from year to year.

In pursuit of that supreme ideal the Commonwealth is moving steadily towards greater harmony between its many creeds, colours and races despite the imperfections by which, like every human institution, it is beset. Already, indeed,

in the last half-century it has proved itself the most effective and progressive association of peoples which history has yet seen; and its ideal of brotherhood embraces the whole world. To all my peoples throughout the Commonwealth I commend that Christmas hope and prayer.

And now I want to say something to my people in New Zealand. Last night a most grievous railway accident took place at Tangiwai which will have brought tragedy into many homes and sorrow into all upon this Christmas day. I know there is no one in New Zealand, and indeed throughout the Commonwealth, who will not join with my husband and me in sending to those who mourn a message of sympathy in their loss. I pray that they and all who have been injured may be comforted and strengthened.

A very young Prince Charles and Princess Anne wait patiently as their mother chats to her Prime Minister, Winston Churchill in 1953.

# 1954

*The Queen's Broadcast came at the end of a year in which Her Majesty and Prince Philip had travelled around the world, from Bermuda to Uganda. As in 1952, The Queen made her broadcast from her study at Sandringham, Norfolk.*

It is now two years since my husband and I spent Christmas with our children. And as we do so today we look back upon a Christmas spent last year in Auckland in hot sunshine, thirteen thousand miles away. Though this was strange for us, we felt at home there, for we were among people who are my own people and whose affectionate greeting I shall remember all my life long. They surrounded us with kindness and friendship, as did all my people throughout the mighty sweep of our world-encircling journey.

Nevertheless, to all of us there is nothing quite like the family gathering in familiar surroundings, centred on the children whose Festival this truly is, in the traditional atmosphere of love and happiness that springs from the enjoyment of simple well-tried things. When it is night and wind and rain beat upon the window, the family is most conscious of the warmth and peacefulness that surround the pleasant fireside. So, our Commonwealth hearth becomes more precious than ever before by the contrast between its homely security and the storm which sometimes seems to be brewing outside, in the darkness of uncertainty and doubt that envelops the whole world.

In the turbulence of this anxious and active world many people are leading uneventful lonely lives. To them dreariness, not disaster, is the enemy. They seldom realise that on their steadfastness, on their ability to withstand the fatigue of dull repetitive work and on their courage in meeting constant small adversities, depend in great measure the happiness and prosperity of the community as a whole.

When we look at the landscape of our life on this earth there is in the minds of all of us a tendency to admire the peaks, and to ignore the foothills and the fertile plain from which they spring. We praise — and rightly — the heroes whose resource and courage shine so brilliantly in moments of crisis. We forget sometimes that behind the wearers of the Victoria or George Cross there stand ranks of unknown, unnamed men and women, willing and able, if the call came, to render valiant service.

We are amazed by the spectacular discoveries in scientific knowledge, which should bring comfort and leisure to millions. We do not always reflect that these things also have rested to some extent on the faithful toil and devotion to duty of the great bulk

of ordinary citizens. The upward course of a nation's history is due, in the long run, to the soundness of heart of its average men and women.

And so it is that this Christmas Day I want to send a special message of encouragement and good cheer to those of you whose lot is cast in dull and unenvied surroundings, to those whose names will never be household words, but to whose work and loyalty we owe so much. May you be proud to remember — as I am myself — how much depends on you and that even when your life seems most monotonous, what you do is always of real value and importance to your fellow men.

I have referred to Christmas as the Children's Festival. But this lovely day is not only a time for family reunions, for paper decorations, for roast turkey and plum pudding. It has, before all, its origin in the homage we pay to a very special Family, who lived long ago in a very ordinary home, in a very unimportant village in the uplands of a small Roman province. Life in such a place might have been uneventful. But the Light, kindled in Bethlehem and then streaming from the cottage window in Nazareth, has illumined the world for two thousand years. It is in the glow of that bright beam that I wish you all a blessed Christmas and a happy New Year!

The Queen filming from the deck of the HMS *Gothic* during the coronation world tour of 1953, with Prince Philip not far behind.

# 1955

*This year saw the retirement of Prime Minister Sir Winston Churchill, with whom The Queen had enjoyed a warm relationship. The theme of her Christmas Broadcast was the Commonwealth of Nations.*

No doubt you have been listening, as I have, to the messages which have been reaching us from all over the world. I always feel that just for these few minutes, the march of history stops while we listen to each other, and think of each other, on Christmas Day.

For my husband and myself and for our children, the year that is passing has added to our store of happy memories. We have spent most of it in this country, and we have enjoyed seeing many parts of Britain which we had not visited before. Now a New Year will soon be upon us, and we are looking forward to seeing something of Nigeria, that great tropical land in Equatorial Africa where more than thirty millions of my people have their homes.

For them and for all of us each New Year is an adventure into the unknown. Year by year, new secrets of nature are being revealed to us by science — secrets of immense power, for good or evil, according to their use. These discoveries resolve some of our problems, but they make others deeper and more immediate. A hundred years ago, our knowledge of the world's surface was by no means complete; today most of the blanks have been filled in. Our present explorations are into new territories of scientific knowledge and into the undeveloped regions of human behaviour. We have still to solve the problem of living peaceably together as peoples and as nations.We shall need the faith and determination of our forebears, when they crossed uncharted seas into the hidden interiors of Africa and Australia, to guide us on our journeys into the undiscovered realms of the human spirit.

In the words of our Poet Laureate:  [John Masefield]

> *Though you have conquered Earth and charted Sea*
> *And planned the courses of all Stars that be,*
> *Adventure on, more wonders are in Thee.*
> *Adventure on, for from the littlest clue*
> *Has come whatever worth man ever knew;*
> *The next to lighten all men may be you.*

Well done, darling! The Queen presents her husband (also the
Windsor Park Team captain) with the Windsor Cup after his polo
team beat India's during the Ascot week tournament.

We must adventure on if we are to make the world a better place. All my peoples of the Commonwealth and Empire have their part to play in this voyage of discovery. We travel all together, just as the Maori tribes sailed all together into the mysterious South Pacific to find New Zealand.

There are certain spiritual values which inspire all of us. We try to express them in our devotion to freedom, which means respect for the individual and equality before the law. Parliamentary Government is also a part of this heritage. We believe in the conception of a Government and Opposition and the right to criticise and defend. All these things are part of the natural life of our free Commonwealth.

Great opportunities lie before us. Indeed a large part of the world looks to the Commonwealth for a lead. We have already gone far towards discovering for ourselves how different nations, from North and South, from East and West, can live together in friendly brotherhood, pooling the resources of each for the benefit of all. Every one of us can also help in this great adventure, for just as the Commonwealth is made up of different nations, so those nations are made up of individuals. The greater the enterprise the more important our personal contribution.

*Year by year, new secrets of nature are being revealed to us by science – secrets of immense power, for good or evil, according to their use.*

The Christmas message to each of us is indivisible; there can be no 'Peace on earth' without 'Goodwill toward men'. Scientists talk of 'chain reaction' — of power releasing yet more power. This principle must be most true when it is applied to the greatest power of all: the power of love.

My beloved grandfather, King George V, in one of his broadcasts when I was a little girl, called upon all his peoples in these words: 'Let each of you be ready and proud to give to his country the service of his work, his mind and his heart.' That is surely the first step to set in motion the 'chain reaction' of the Powers of Light, to illuminate the new age ahead of us. And the second step is this: to understand with sympathy the point of view of others, within our own countries and in the Commonwealth, as well as those outside it. In this way we can bring our unlimited spiritual resources to bear upon the world.

As this Christmas passes by, and time resumes its march, let us resolve that the spirit of Christmas shall stay with us as we journey into the unknown year that lies ahead.

# 1956

*On Christmas Day The Duke of Edinburgh was away on a voyage around the Commonwealth on HMY* Britannia. *He spoke to The Queen from the* Royal Yacht *before she made her live Christmas Broadcast.*

Once again messages of Christmas greeting have been exchanged around the world. From all parts of the Commonwealth, and from the remote and lonely spaces of Antarctica, words and thoughts, taking their inspiration from the birth of the child in Bethlehem long ago, have been carried between us upon the invisible wings of twentieth-century science.

Neither the long and troubled centuries that have passed since that child was born, nor the complex scientific developments of our age, have done anything to dim the simple joy and bright hope we all feel when we celebrate his birthday. That joy and hope find their most complete fulfilment within the loving circle of a united family.

You will understand me, therefore, when I tell you that of all the voices we have heard this afternoon none has given my children and myself greater joy than that of my husband. To him I say: 'From all the members of the family gathered here today our very best good wishes go out to you and to every one on board Britannia, as you voyage together in the far Southern seas. Happy Christmas from us all.'

Of course it is sad for us to be separated on this day, and of course we look forward to the moment when we shall all again be together. Yet my husband's absence at this time has made me even more aware than I was before of my own good fortune in being one of a united family. With that consciousness in mind, I would like to send a special message of hope and encouragement to all who are not so blessed, or for any reason cannot be with those they love today: to the sick who cannot be at home; to all who serve their country in foreign lands, or whose duty keeps them upon the oceans; and to every man or woman whose destiny it is to walk through life alone.

Particularly on this day of the family festival let us remember those who — like the Holy Family before them — have been driven from their homes by war or violence. We call them 'refugees': let us give them a true refuge: let us see that for them and their children there is room at the Inn.

If my husband cannot be at home on Christmas Day, I could not wish for a better reason than that he should be travelling in other parts of the Commonwealth. On his

The Queen visits the people of a leper community at Oji River near Enugu during a state visit to eastern Nigeria in February. By the 1950s, Nigeria was ahead of many countries in treating the disease, now known as Hansen's disease, although sufferers were still stigmatised.

journey he has returned to many places that we have already visited together, and he has been to others that I have never seen. On the voyage back to England he will call at some of the least accessible parts of the world, those islands of the South Atlantic separated from us by immense stretches of the ocean, yet linked to us with bonds of brotherhood and trust.

One idea above all others has been the mainspring of this journey. It is the wish to foster, and advance, concord and understanding within the Commonwealth. No purpose comes nearer to my own desires, for I believe that the way in which our Commonwealth is developing represents one of the most hopeful and imaginative experiments in international affairs that the world has ever seen. If, as its Head, I can make any real personal contribution towards its progress, it must surely be to promote its unity.

We talk of ourselves as a 'family of nations', and perhaps our relations with one another are not so very different from those which exist between members of any family. We all know that these are not always easy, for there is no law within a family which binds its members to think, or act, or be alike. And surely it is this very

*We talk of ourselves as a 'family of nations', and perhaps our relations with one another are not so very different from those which exist between members of any family. We all know that these are not always easy...*

freedom of choice and decision which gives exceptional value to friendship in times of stress and disagreement. Such friendship is a gift for which we are truly and rightly grateful. None the less, deep and acute differences, involving both intellect and emotion, are bound to arise between members of a family and also between friend and friend, and there is neither virtue nor value in pretending that they do not. In all such differences, however, there comes a moment when, for the sake of ultimate harmony, the healing power of tolerance, comradeship and love must be allowed to play its part.

I speak of a tolerance that is not indifference, but is rather a willingness to recognise the possibility of right in others; of a comradeship that is not just a sentimental memory of good days past, but the certainty that the tried and staunch friends of yesterday are still in truth the same people today; of a love that can rise above anger and is ready to forgive.

That each one of us should give this power a chance to do its work is my heartfelt message to you all upon this Christmas Day. I can think of no better resolve to make, nor any better day on which to make it. Let us remember this during our festivities, for it is part of the Christmas message — "Goodwill toward men". I wish you all a Happy Christmas and a Happy New Year.

# 1957

*This year millions of people saw, as well as heard The Queen as her Christmas Broadcast was televised for the first time.  She spoke live from the Long Library at Sandringham, family photographs clearly visible on her desk.*

Twenty-five years ago my grandfather broadcast the first of these Christmas messages. Today is another landmark because television has made it possible for many of you to see me in your homes on Christmas Day. My own family often gather round to watch television as they are this moment, and that is how I imagine you now.

I very much hope that this new medium will make my Christmas message more personal and direct. It is inevitable that I should seem a rather remote figure to many of you. A successor to the Kings and Queens of history; someone whose face may be familiar in newspapers and films but who never really touches your personal lives. But now at least for a few minutes I welcome you to the peace of my own home.

That it is possible for some of you to see me today is just another example of the speed at which things are changing all around us. Because of these changes I am not surprised that many people feel lost and unable to decide what to hold on to and what to discard. How to take advantage of the new life without losing the best of the old.

But it is not the new inventions which are the difficulty. The trouble is caused by unthinking people who carelessly throw away ageless ideals as if they were old and outworn machinery. They would have religion thrown aside, morality in personal and public life made meaningless, honesty counted as foolishness and self-interest set up in place of self-restraint.

At this critical moment in our history we will certainly lose the trust and respect of the world if we just abandon those fundamental principles which guided the men and women who built the greatness of this country and Commonwealth. Today we need a special kind of courage, not the kind needed in battle but a kind which makes us stand up for everything that we know is right, everything that is true and honest. We need the kind of courage that can withstand the subtle corruption of the cynics so that we can show the world that we are not afraid of the future. It has always been easy to hate and destroy. To build and to cherish is much more difficult. That is why we can take a pride in the new Commonwealth we are building.

As a friend of the royal family, the photographer Antony Armstrong-Jones (later the Earl of Snowdon) was able to capture intimate moments such as this, as The Queen reads to seven-year-old Princess Anne in the gardens of Buckingham Palace.

*Today we need a special kind of courage, not the kind needed in battle but a kind which makes us stand up for everything that we know is right, everything that is true and honest.*

This year Ghana and Malaya joined our brotherhood. Both these countries are now entirely self-governing. Both achieved their new status amicably and peacefully. This advance is a wonderful tribute to the efforts of men of goodwill who have worked together as friends, and I welcome these two countries with all my heart.

Last October I opened the new Canadian Parliament, and as you know this was the first time that any Sovereign had done so in Ottawa. Once again I was overwhelmed by the loyalty and enthusiasm of my Canadian people. Also during 1957 my husband and I paid visits to Portugal, France, Denmark and the United States of America. In each case the arrangements and formalities were managed with great skill but no one could have 'managed' the welcome we received from the people.

In each country I was welcomed as Head of the Commonwealth and as your representative. These nations are our friends largely because we have always tried to do our best to be honest and kindly and because we have tried to stand up for what we believe to be right.

*Opposite above:* The Queen and Prince Philip during a royal visit to Portugal in February 1957 — at sea and at the theatre; where they were accompanied by Portuguese heads of state.

In the old days the monarch led his soldiers on the battlefield and his leadership at all times was close and personal. Today things are very different. I cannot lead you into battle, I do not give you laws or administer justice but I can do something else, I can give you my heart and my devotion to these old islands and to all the peoples of our brotherhood of nations. I believe in our qualities and in our strength, I believe that together we can set an example to the world which will encourage upright people everywhere.

I would like to read you a few lines from *Pilgrim's Progress*, because I am sure we can say with Mr Valiant for Truth, these words:

> *Though with great difficulty I am got hither, yet now I do not repent me of all the trouble I have been at to arrive where I am. My sword I give to him that shall succeed me in my pilgrimage and my courage and skill to him that can get it. My marks and scars I carry with me, to be a witness for me that I have fought his battles who now will be my rewarder.*

I hope that 1958 may bring you God's blessing and all the things you long for. And so I wish you all, young and old, wherever you may be, all the fun and enjoyment, and the peace of a very happy Christmas.

# 1958

*The Queen's Christmas Broadcast in 1958 focused on some of the journeys soon to be made around the Commonwealth by herself and members of the Royal Family.*

Every year I look forward to opening the letters, parcels and telegrams that come to me from all parts of the world. My husband and children join me in thanking all of you who have sent us your good wishes for Christmas and the New Year.

Some of you have written to say that you would like to see our children on television this afternoon. We value your interest in them and I can assure you that we have thought about this a great deal before deciding against it. We would like our son and daughter to grow up as normally as possible so that they will be able to serve you and the Commonwealth faithfully and well when they are old enough to do so. We believe that public life is not a fair burden to place on growing children. I'm sure that all of you who are parents will understand.

Very soon now we shall be entering into the uncertainty and promise of a new year. I hope very much that it proves to be a year of progress and happiness for us all. My family and I are looking forward to it, especially because many of us will be travelling to different parts of the world and hope to see more of you than ever before. In three weeks' time my husband goes to India and Pakistan and then on across the Pacific. My mother is going to East Africa and my uncle, The Duke of Gloucester, and his wife, will be travelling as my representatives to Nigeria. My aunt, The Duchess of Kent, and my cousin, Princess Alexandra, are also undertaking long journeys. Together they will be visiting Central and South America in the spring and, later, Princess Alexandra goes to Australia to attend the centenary celebrations of the state of Queensland.

In June, my husband and I will be going to Canada once again. You'll remember that my sister, Princess Margaret, was there earlier this year. This time we go primarily to open the great St. Lawrence Seaway, but we shall be visiting many other parts of the country as well. Lastly — towards the end of the year — we are going to Ghana and on our way back we intend to visit my people in Sierra Leone and the Gambia. So, between us, we are going to many parts of the world. We have no plans for space travel — at the moment.

To Christians all over the world, Christmas is an occasion for family gatherings and celebrations, for presents and parties, for friendship and good will. To many of my

Much to the admiration of the miners, The Queen donned overalls and descended the mine at the Rothes Colliery, Fife, during a royal visit to Scotland.

people Christmas doesn't have the same religious significance, but friendship and good will are common to us all. So it's a good time to remember those around us who are far from home, feeling perhaps strange and lonely. My own thoughts are with the men and women and children from other parts of the Commonwealth who have come to live and work in the great cities of this country and may well be missing the warmth and sunshine of their homelands.

In recent years the Commonwealth countries have been making a great co-operative effort to raise standards of living. Even so, the pace of our everyday life has been such that there has hardly been time to enjoy the things which appeal to men's minds and which make life a full experience. After all, our standard of living has a spiritual as well as a material aspect. The genius of scientists, inventors and engineers can make life more comfortable and prosperous. But throughout history the spiritual and intellectual aspirations of mankind have been inspired by prophets and dreamers, philosophers, men of ideas and poets, artists in paint, sculpture and music, the whole company who challenge and encourage or who entertain and give pleasure. To their number I would add the teachers in Church, school and university, whose enormous job it is to awaken the minds of the younger generations and instil into them the essence of our accumulated civilisation.

I am sure that many of you have thought about these things before, but it seems to me that Christmas is just the time to be grateful to those who add fullness to our lives. Even so, we need something more. We all need the kind of security that one gets from a happy and united family.

# 1959

*The Queen's Christmas Broadcast in 1959 took the form of a pre-recorded radio message instead of a television broadcast. The Queen was pregnant with her third child, Prince Andrew, who was born the following February.*

I do not want Christmas to pass by without sending my best wishes for a happy day to all of you who may be listening, and especially to my own peoples in the Commonwealth. Wherever you are and whatever you may be doing, you have my constant interest and affection.

I am particularly grateful to the many kind people all over the world who have sent me their good wishes at this time. I am glad to have this chance to thank you all very warmly indeed. As the old year passes, let us celebrate Christmas with thanksgiving and carry its message of peace and good will into the year ahead. All of us at Sandringham wish you a very happy Christmas. May God bless you all.

# 1960

*In her Christmas Broadcast The Queen recalled an eventful year. She gave birth
to her third child, Prince Andrew, her sister Princess Margaret married society
photographer Antony Armstrong-Jones and Nigeria gained independence, while
remaining part of the Commonwealth.*

I am glad at Christmas time to have this opportunity of speaking directly to all the
peoples of the Commonwealth and of sending you my good wishes. My husband
and our children, together with the other members of our family, join me in wishing
every one of you a happy Christmas and a prosperous new year.

I make no excuse for telling you once again that the kind messages which reach us
from all over the world at this season give us great pleasure and encouragement. This
year I was delighted to get so many when my second son was born. The telegrams
and letters which came flooding in at that time made me feel very close to all the
family groups throughout the Commonwealth.

It is this feeling of personal association which gives the peoples of the
Commonwealth countries that special relationship, one to another, which others
find so difficult to understand. It is because of this that my husband and I are so
greatly looking forward to our visits to India and Pakistan early next year and later
on to Ghana, Sierra Leone and the Gambia.

By no stretch of the imagination can 1960 be described as a happy or successful year
for mankind. Arguments and strained relations, as well as natural disasters, have
all helped to produce an atmosphere of tension and uncertainty all over the world.
Although the causes are beyond the control of individuals, we can at least
influence the future by our everyday behaviour. It is at times of change, disorder and
uncertainty that we should cling most strongly to all those principles which we
know to be right and good.

*Opposite;* A peaceful moment during
a family picnic in the grounds of
Balmoral in September 1960, with a
baby Prince Andrew being admired
by his elder brother and sister.

*Co-operation between Commonwealth countries grows*
*every year and the understanding and mutual appreciation*
*which is developing at the same time is one of the really*
*bright spots in the world today.*

Civilisation as we know it, or would like it to be, depends upon a constant striving towards better things. In times of stress, such as we are living through, only a determined effort by men and women of good will everywhere can halt and reverse a growing tendency towards violence and disintegration.

Despite the difficulties there are encouraging signs. For instance in Africa, Nigeria has gone through the process of achieving full self-government in peace and good will. This great nation of thirty million people has decided to remain a member of our Commonwealth and I know that her influence will be most valuable as the future unfolds in other parts of Africa.

Then, again, co-operation between Commonwealth countries grows every year and the understanding and mutual appreciation which is developing at the same time is one of the really bright spots in the world today. Although the contribution which any one person can make is small, it is real and important. Whether you live in one of the rapidly developing countries of the Commonwealth or whether you find yourself in one of the older countries, the work of mutual help and the increase of mutual understanding cannot fail to be personally satisfying and of real service to the future.

May the months ahead bring you joy and the peace and happiness which we so much desire. Happy Christmas. God bless you all.

*Opposite above:* The announcement of the engagement of The Queen's younger sister Princess Margaret to society photographer Antony Armstrong-Jones in February came as quite a surprise, as their courtship had been kept a secret since they met in 1958; *below:* the Royal Family, with toddler Prince Andrew, on the roof of Balmoral Castle in October 1960.

# 1961

*In 1961 The Queen carried out a six-week tour of India, Pakistan, Nepal and Iran, visiting the Taj Mahal and laying a wreath on Mahatma Gandhi's monument. She also paid a visit to the Vatican City, calling on Pope John XXIII. In her Christmas Broadcast, made from Buckingham Palace, The Queen reflected on these travels.*

Every year at this time the whole Christian world celebrates the birth of the founder of our faith. It is traditionally the time for family reunions, present-giving and children's parties. A welcome escape, in fact, from the harsh realities of this troubled world and it is just in times like these, times of tension and anxieties, that the simple story and message of Christmas is most relevant.

The story is of a poor man and his wife who took refuge at night in a stable, where a child was born and laid in the manger. Nothing very spectacular, and yet the event was greeted with that triumphant song: 'Glory to God in the highest, and on earth peace, goodwill towards men.'

For that child was to show that there is nothing in heaven and earth that cannot be achieved by faith and by love and service to one's neighbour. Christmas may be a Christian festival, but its message goes out to all men and it is echoed by all men of understanding and goodwill everywhere.

During this last year I have been able to visit many countries: some were members of the Commonwealth and some were not. In all of them I was shown a genuine kindness and affection which touched me deeply and showed, I think, that the British people are looked upon as friends in many parts of the world. In Asia and in Africa we were made aware of the great volume of good will and friendship that exists between all the varied peoples who profess different faiths and who make up our Commonwealth family. To them, their Christian brethren send a message of hope and encouragement this Christmas.

It goes also to the quiet people who fight prejudice by example, who stick to standards and ideals in face of persecution; who make real sacrifices in order to help and serve their neighbours.

'Oh hush the noise, ye men of strife, and hear the angels sing.' The words of this old carol mean even more today than when they were first written.

We can only dispel the clouds of anxiety by the patient and determined efforts of us all. It cannot be done by condemning the past or by contracting out of the present. Angry words and accusations certainly don't do any good, however justified they may be.

It is natural that the younger generation should lose patience with their elders, for their seeming failure to bring some order and security to the world. But things will not get any better if young people merely express themselves by indifference or by revulsion against what they regard as an out-of-date order of things. The world desperately needs their vigour, their determination and their service to their fellow men. The opportunities are there and the reward is the satisfaction of truly unselfish work.

To both young and old I send my very best wishes and, as the carol says, may we all hear the angels sing in the coming year. A very happy Christmas to you all.

The Queen during a royal tour of India. She is pictured in Benares, now Uttar Pradesh, in the north east of the country. The tour also included a visit to neighbouring Nepal.

# 1962~1971

## *The* SWINGING SIXTIES

Queen Elizabeth II during her visit to HMS Ganges
at Shotleyy in Suffolk.

Elizabeth II was mother to three children: Prince Charles (born 1948), HRH Princess Anne (1950) and HRH Prince Andrew (born 1960), welcoming her fourth child, HRH Prince Edward, in 1964. The Queen was just 22 when Prince Charles was born, and when he ascends the throne he will be the oldest British monarch ever to be crowned. The oldest previously appointed had been William IV, who was born in 1765 but didn't accede the throne until 1830, when he was aged 64 years and 163 days. He enjoyed just seven years on the throne. In this decade, The Queen welcomed four Prime Minsters: Harold Macmillan (1957-63) and Alec Douglas-Home (1963-64), Harold Wilson (1964-70) and Edward Heath (1970-74).

The 'swinging' sixties, as the decade became known, finally put the 1950s to bed. It was dominated by the multi-talented Beatles, who formed in 1962; the Profumo Affair, the Great Train Robbery, the coldest winter since 1947 and the reckless Beeching Report (which proposed reshaping our railways), all in 1963. Sir Winston Churchill's death in 1965 and the spectacular 1966 World Cup England soccer win showcased the nation in many different guises. British fashion designer Mary Quant introduced tiny shorts (precursors of the 70's hotpants) and miniskirts, which made Chelsea 'cool' and the hippest place to be. Quant was eventually commissioned to design the interior of the Mini 1000 car, which was somehow appropriate, given she had taken the name of her eponymous skirt from the original Mini created by Sir Alec Issigonis in 1959. But the catastrophic collapse in 1966 of the colliery tip at Aberfan in south Wales, which killed 28 adults and 116 children, cast a shadow over the nation, as did the 66 deaths during a football match crush at Ibrox Park, Glasgow, in 1971.

Television and radio were in change mode and together they threatened the future of cinemas that were behind the curve, with hundreds being closed as a result. After a bumpy start, ITV's regional channel structure was beginning to threaten the hegemony of the BBC, which had to be creative in order to compete with the increasing success of the regional channels. When BBC2 was launched in 1964, the main channel became known as BBC1. BBC2's opening night was on 20 April, but a serious power cut wiped the entire schedule. Colour television was first introduced with the coverage of Wimbledon on 1 July 1967, on BBC1.

By the end of the decade almost 95 per cent of the population either owned or rented a television set, with half of them paying the new £10 annual colour licence fee (black-and-white remained at £5). Meanwhile, BBC Radio was being seriously threatened by offshore illegal radio stations like Radio Caroline and Radio London (both started in 1964), based on boats were anchored outside the UK's territorial waters in the North Sea. The BBC's eventually answer in 1967 was to create a new radio station, Radio 1, and to rebrand its existing national radio stations, with the Light Programme becoming Radio 2; Third Programme Radio 3; and the Home Service Radio 4.

Some of the programmes launched on BBC remain favourites even now. These included *Z Cars* and *Steptoe and Son* (1962); *Dr Who* (1963; *Match of the Day* (1964), and *Not Only…But Also (1965),* which occasionally featured John Lennon alongside hosts Peter Cooke and Dudley Moore. Ken Loach's landmark television play about homelessness, *Cathy Come Home* (1966), attracted 12 million viewers, an extraordinary number for a drama documentary. *Beyond the Fringe,* a British comedy stage revue was first performed on stage at the Edinburgh Festival in 1960. It went on to play in London's West End and then in America. It kick-started a trend for shows that were humorous, wildly eccentric and offered a satirical view of the recent past. Without its creators Peter Cooke, Dudley Moore, Alan Bennett and Jonathan Miller there would have been no *That Was the Week That Was* (1962), *At Last the 1948 Show* (1967) and *Monty Python's Flying Circus* (1969-forever). And without the trailblazing *The Goons* radio show, which launched in 1951 and starred Spike Milligan, Peter Sellars, Harry Secombe, and comedy TV series *It's a Square World,* which started in 1960 and starred the madcap Michael Bentine, it would have been unlikely that the worldwide 'Fringe' festival would have become the success it is today.

There were a flux of other festivals including the Isle of Wight in the summer of 1968, which attracted 10,000 to a farmer's field to see Jimi Hendrix, The Doors, Leonard Cohen, Chicago and Jethro Tull. A year later on a dairy farm outside New York, Woodstock attracted over 400,000. Later four million would claim they were there. And not to be outdone, the Pilton Pops, Folk and Blues Festival was launched in 1970. Better known today as the Hay Festival it was founded by Rhoda, Norman and Peter Florence. Hay 'fever' has spread its festivals to fifteen other countries.

There was further illustration of how the sixties represented a change to our lives with the publication of Anthony Burgess's dystopian novel *A Clockwork Orange;* John Robinson, Bishop of Woolwich's controversial critique of Christian theology, *Honest to God;* E.P. Thompson's social history book, *The Making of the Working Class* and zoologist Desmond Morris's *The Naked Ape.* Terence Conran opened his first contemporary homeware store, Habitat, in Fulham, west London. In 1962, British orthopaedic surgeon Sir John Charnley performed the first total hip replacement at Wrightington Hospital near Wigan, Greater Manchester. In 1967, cardiac surgeon Christiaan Barnard performed the first human-to-human heart transplant in the South Africa. NASA's

Apollo 11 space rocket landed on the moon in 1969 and Neil Armstrong uttered the now legendary phrase: 'That's one small step for a man, one giant leap for mankind.' The landing was seen by a worldwide television audience of 650 million people. In contrast, on planet Earth, Norwegian adventurer and ethnographer Thor Heyerdahl, known from his previous *Kon-Tiki* raft expedition in 1947, sailed from Morocco to Barbados in 1970, in a reed boat called *Ra II*. His work was a game-changer in contradicting the perceived academic wisdom about cultural development, showing how ancient populations were able to make long sea voyages and connect to different groups of people. Somehow, the Nobel Prize committee failed to appreciate his genius.

Politician Sir Winston Churchill, who was never short of a bon mot (he *had* won a Nobel Prize for Literature in 1953), had a special relationship with the public during the dark years of the early part of World War II.  When he died in in 1965, The Queen decreed his body should lie in state at Westminster Hall in Parliament for three days. During that time, more than 320,000 mourners passed his coffin, queuing for hours and hours to pay their respects. Lines over a mile long were recorded. Churchill's funeral took place at St Paul's Cathedral four days later.

World leaders also paid tribute to the great wartime leader. Prime Minister Harold Wilson declared :

*Sir Winston will be mourned all over the world by all who owe so much to him. He is now at peace after a life in which he created history and which will be remembered as long as history is read.*

In a BBC poll in 2002, Sir Winston Churchill was voted the greatest Briton. Maybe, his death enabled the nation to move on.

# 1962

*The 1960s were a decade of exciting technological development. In her Christmas Broadcast The Queen praised the launch of the first active communications satellite, Telstar, that made it possible to broadcast news and images around the world almost instantly.*

### A Merry Christmas and a Happy New Year.

There is something wonderful in the way these old familiar warm-hearted words of the traditional Christmas message never seem to grow stale. Surely it is because the family festival is like a firm landmark in the stormy seas of modern life. Year by year, our families change and grow up. So does our Commonwealth family. This year Jamaica, Trinidad and Tobago and Uganda have joined the circle as full members and we wish them all good fortune.

My husband and I are greatly looking forward to revisiting New Zealand and Australia in the New Year. We shall meet many old friends and make new ones and we shall be very interested to see some of the many new developments which have taken place since I was last there nine years ago. In spite of all the changes of the modern world and the many stresses and strains involved, the feeling of a special relationship between the ordinary people of the older Commonwealth countries will never be weakened. This feeling is rapidly spreading throughout the newer members and in its turn will help us to realise the ideal of human brotherhood.

In the ideal of the Commonwealth we have been entrusted with something very special. We have in our hands a most potent force for good, and one of the true unifying bonds in this torn world. Let us keep faith with the ideal we know to be right and be ambitious for the good of all men.

Mankind continues to achieve wonders in technical and space research but in the western world perhaps the launching of *Telstar* has captured the imagination most vividly. This tiny satellite has become the invisible focus of a million eyes. *Telstar*, and her sister satellites as they arise, can now show the world to the world just as it is in its daily life. What a wonderfully exciting prospect and perhaps it will make us stop and think about what sort of picture we are presenting to each other.

Wise men since the beginning of time have studied the skies. Whatever our faith, we can all follow a star — indeed we must follow one if the immensity of the future opening before us is not to dazzle our eyes and dissipate our sense of direction.

How is it, people wonder, that we are forever seeking new worlds to conquer before we have properly put our own house in order. Some people are uncertain which star to follow, or if any star is worth following at all. What is it all for, they ask, if you can bounce a telephone conversation or a television picture through the skies and across the world, yet still find lonely people living in the same street?

Following a star has many meanings; it can mean the religious man's approach to God or the hopes of parents for their children, or the ambition of young men and women, or the devotion of old countries like ours to well-tried ideals of toleration and justice, with no distinction of race or creed.

The wise men of old followed a star: modern man has built one. But unless the message of this new star is the same as theirs our wisdom will count for nought. Now we can all say the world is my neighbour and it is only in serving one another that we can reach for the stars.

The Queen inspects immaculate Chelsea Pensioners on Founders' Day at the Royal Hospital in London in May. Today over 300 British army veterans, both men and women, live in sheltered accommodation at the Hospital.

# 1963

*The Queen's Christmas Broadcast in 1963 was made by radio, as she was
pregnant with her fourth child, Prince Edward, who was born in
March of the following year.*

Since my last message of Christmas greetings to you all, the world has witnessed many great events and sweeping changes, but they are already part of the long record of history.

Now, as ever, the important time for mankind is the future; the coming years are full of hope and promise and their course can still be shaped by our will and action. The message of Christmas remains the same; but humanity can only progress if we are all truly ambitious for what is good and honourable. We know the reward is peace on earth, goodwill toward men, but we cannot win it without determination and concerted effort.

One such concerted effort has been the campaign to free the world from hunger. I am very happy to know that the people of the Commonwealth have responded so generously to this campaign.

Much has been achieved but there is still much to do and on this day of reunions and festivities in the glow of Christmas, let us remember the many undernourished people, young and old, scattered throughout the world. All my family joins me in sending every one of you best wishes for Christmas and may God's blessing be with you in the coming year.

*Opposite:* In June the newly enlarged royal family wave from balcony during Trooping of the Colour. The Queen holds baby Edward, born in March.

# 1964

*The Queen's Christmas Broadcast in 1964 addressed the important role of the Commonwealth in a year in which anti-apartheid leader Nelson Mandela was jailed in South Africa, and Indian Prime Minister Jawaharlal Nehru died.*

As I begin my Christmas Broadcast to you, the people of Great Britain and of the other Commonwealth countries, my mind travels far away, and for one moment I seem to be with you in many countries, which are now almost as familiar as my own native land. To you all, my family and I send our affectionate greetings and hope that your Christmas is a happy one.

Let us think for a moment about this great Commonwealth. What is this wealth, which we have in common and which is so much more than our collective resources, massive though they are?

I know that life is hard for many. The problems which face mankind often seem to defy solution. Some of our Commonwealth friends overseas are grappling with difficulties

unknown in a complex industrial country such as Great Britain. There are difficulties of over-population, there is hunger, and drought and lack of power. There are yearly tens of thousands of young people flocking into schools, seeking education.

I welcome the chance of hearing more about these problems when individual Ministers from the Commonwealth come to this country, and also on such special occasions as the Prime Ministers' Meetings. At moments like this I have the benefit, not only of getting to know some of my Prime Ministers better, but also of welcoming leaders from the new nations of the Commonwealth.

*All of us who have been blessed with young families know from long experience that when one's house is at its noisiest, there is often less cause for anxiety.*

I value very highly these meetings, which allow me to draw on the wisdom of such a representative gathering. I believe that in God's good time all the peoples of our Commonwealth, working side by side, will attain prosperity.

The thread which runs through our Commonwealth is love of freedom, and it is perhaps in this, more than in anything else, that our real wealth lies. Now the word 'freedom', like the word 'democracy', is a simple one implying a simple idea, and yet freedom, to be effective, must be disciplined.

Absolute freedom is a state unknown to the historian. The many ancient institutions and traditions which we have inherited, and which are familiar to us all, provide a framework and a dignified background to our way of life. If it is not to degenerate, freedom must be maintained by a thousand invisible forces, self-discipline, the Common Law, the right of citizens to assemble, and to speak and argue. We do not wish to impose a particular form of Government on any peoples in the world; we merely say, 'This is what we do; we know it's not perfect, but it is the best system that we have been able to create after many centuries of trial and error.'

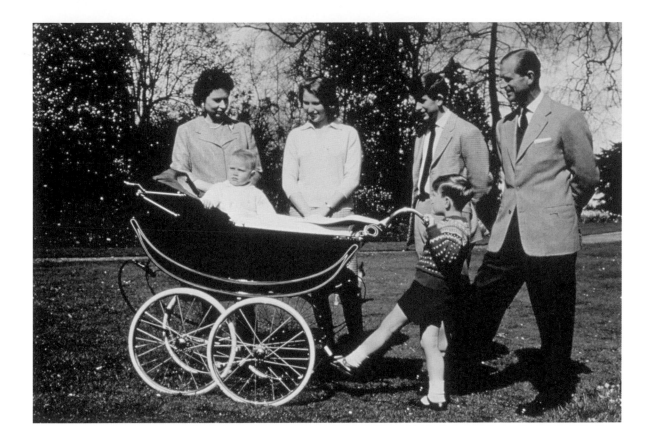

All of us who have been blessed with young families know from long experience that when one's house is at its noisiest, there is often less cause for anxiety. The creaking of a ship in a heavy sea is music in the ears of the captain on the bridge. In fact little is static and without movement there can be no progress.

Some speak today as though the age of adventure and initiative is past. On the contrary, never have the challenges been greater or more urgent. The fight against poverty, malnutrition and ignorance is harder than ever, and we must do all in our power to see that science is directed towards solving these problems.

I would like to say one more word to the young people of the Commonwealth. Upon you rests our hope for the future. You young people are needed; there is a great task ahead of you - the building of a new world. You have brains and courage, imagination and humanity; direct them to the things that have to be achieved in this century, if mankind is to live together in happiness and prosperity.

The Royal Family, with a baby Prince Edward, enjoying fresh air at Windsor on The Queen's thirty-ninth birthday in 1964.

# 14 May 1965
# KENNEDY MEMORIAL

*Following the assassination of President John F. Kennedy, the British Government
decided to commemorate his life with a monument at Runneymede, Windsor.
At the inauguration ceremony in 1965 The Queen spoke movingly of the
shared grief of our two nations.*

Here at Runnymede 750 years ago Magna Carta was signed. Among our earliest
Statutes, it has rightly been regarded as the cornerstone of those liberties which
later became enshrined in our system of democratic government under the rule of law.
This is a part of the heritage which the people of the United States of America share
with us. Therefore it is altogether fitting that this should be the site of Britain's
memorial to the late President John F. Kennedy, for, as leader of his great nation, he
championed liberty in an age when its very foundations were being threatened on a
universal scale.

We all recall how he welcomed this challenge and gloried in the fact that to his
generation had been given the task of defending liberty in such a time of trial. His
readiness to shoulder the burden and the passionate enthusiasm which he brought
to his labours gave courage, inspiration, and, above all, new hope not only to
Americans but to all America's friends.

Nowhere was this more true than here in these Islands. With all their hearts, my
people shared his triumphs, grieved at his reverses and wept at his death.

President Kennedy, together with his family, had many ties with our country. He
and they lived among us in that doom-laden period which led up to the outbreak
of war. The experience of those days led him to write, when still a young man, a
most perceptive analysis of the predicament in which Britain found herself. Ever
after he maintained a deep and steady interest in the affairs of this nation whose
history and literature he knew and loved so well.  His elder brother, flying from these
shores on a hazardous mission, was killed in our common struggle against the evil
forces of a cruel tyranny.  A dearly-loved sister lies buried in an English churchyard.
Bonds like these cannot be broken and his abiding affection for Britain engendered
an equal response from this side of the Atlantic.

The unprecedented intensity of that wave of grief, mixed with something akin
to despair, which swept over our people at the news of President Kennedy's

assassination, was a measure of the extent to which we recognised what he had already accomplished, and of the high hopes that rode with him in a future that was not to be.

He was a man valiant in war, but no one understood better than he that, if total war were to come again, all the finest achievements of the human race would be utterly consumed in the nuclear holocaust. He therefore sought tenaciously for a peace which, as he put it, would enable 'men and nations to grow and to hope and to build a better life for their children – not merely peace for Americans, but peace for all men and women; not merely peace in our time but peace for all time.'

Abroad, peace for a shrinking world; at home, a just and compassionate society. These were the themes of his Presidency. But it is his own example as a man that we remember today; his courage, both moral and physical; his dedication to public service; the distinction of heart and mind, the joyful enthusiasm, the wit and style which he brought to all he did; his love of liberty and of his fellow men. All these will continue to inspire us and the generations who succeed us and all those who share the noble traditions of freemen evoked by the name of Runnymede.

This acre of English soil is now bequeathed in perpetuity to the American people in memory of President John Fitzgerald Kennedy who in death my people still mourn and whom in life they loved and admired.

The Queen gives a speech during the visit of presidential candidate Robert Kennedy, his widowed sister-in-law Jacqueline Kennedy and her children at Runnymede, Windsor in May, where The Queen unveiled a monument to President John F Kennedy, assassinated two years previously.

# 1965

*The Queen took the family, in its widest sense as the theme of her Christmas Broadcast, reminding us that despite all our material wealth, the family remains as the focal point of our existence.*

Every year the familiar pattern of Christmas unfolds. The sights and the customs and festivities may seem very much the same from one year to another, and yet to families and individuals each Christmas is slightly different.

Children grow and presents for them change. It may be the first Christmas for many as husband and wife, or the first Christmas with grandchildren. Some may be far from home, and others lonely or sick, yet Christmas always remains as the great family festival: a festival which we owe to that family long ago which spent this time in extreme adversity and discomfort.

I think we should remember that in spite of all the scientific advances and great improvements in our material welfare, the family remains as the focal point of our existence. There is overwhelming evidence that those who cannot experience full and happy family life for some reason or another are deprived of a great stabilising influence in their lives.

At Christmas we are also reminded that it is the time of peace on earth and goodwill towards men. Yet we are all only too well aware of the tragic fighting, hatred and ill-will in so many parts of the world. Because of this, cynics may shrug off the Christmas message as a waste of time, but that is only the gloomy side of the picture; there are also brighter and more hopeful signs. The great churches of the world are coming to understand each other better and to recognise that without their inspiration and great ideals mankind will be smothered by its own material wealth. We must have dreams and ambitions for peace and goodwill and they must be proclaimed.

Perhaps the most practical demonstration of goodwill towards men is to be found in the growing practice among young people to give some form of voluntary service to others. In Britain and throughout the world they are coming forward to help old people or to serve in every kind of capacity where they may be needed at home and overseas. A new army is on the march, which holds out the brightest hopes for all mankind. It serves in international work camps, in areas hit by natural disasters or emergencies and in helping the poor, the backward or the hungry.

'Peace on Earth' - we may not have it at the moment, we may never have it completely, but we will certainly achieve nothing unless we go on trying to remove the causes of conflict between peoples and nations.

'Goodwill towards men' is not a hollow phrase. Goodwill exists, and when there is an opportunity to show it in practical form we know what wonderful things it can achieve. To deny this Christmas message is to admit defeat and to give up hope. It is a rejection of everything that makes life worth living, and what is far worse it offers nothing in its place.

In fact it is just because there are so many conflicts in the world today that we should reaffirm our hopes and beliefs in a more peaceful and a more friendly world in the future. This is just the moment to remind ourselves that we can all find some practical way to serve others and help to create a better understanding between people. To each one of you I wish a very happy Christmas and if throughout the Commonwealth we can all make a sustained effort, perhaps Christmas next year will be a much happier one for many more people.

The Queen at Carisbrooke Castle on the Isle of Wight, where she installed Earl Mountbatten of Burma as Governor of the island in July.

# 1966

*In her Christmas Broadcast of 1966, in a decade which saw great changes for women, The Queen spoke about the increasingly prominent and important role played by women in society as they challenge ignorance and prejudice.*

Ever since the first Christmas when the three wise men brought their presents, Christians all over the world have kept up this kindly custom. Even if the presents we give each other at Christmas-time may only be intended to give momentary pleasure, they do also reflect one all important lesson. Society cannot hope for a just and peaceful civilisation unless each individual feels the need to be concerned about his fellows.

All the great works of charity and all humanitarian legislation have always been inspired by a flame of compassion which has burnt brightly in the hearts of men and women. Mankind has many blemishes, but deep down in every human soul there is a store of goodwill waiting to be called upon.

This year I should like to speak especially to women. In many countries custom has decreed that women should play a minor part in public affairs. It is difficult to realise that it was less than fifty years ago that women in Britain were first given the vote, but Parliament was first asked to grant this one hundred years ago.

*The struggles against inhuman prejudice, against squalor, ignorance and disease, have always owed a great deal to the determination and tenacity of women.*

Yet, in spite of these disabilities, it has been women who have breathed gentleness and care into the harsh progress of mankind. The struggles against inhuman prejudice, against squalor, ignorance, and disease, have always owed a great deal to the determination and tenacity of women. The devotion of nuns and nurses, the care of mothers and wives, the service of teachers, and the conviction of reformers are the real and enduring presents which women have always given.

In the modern world the opportunities for women to give something of value to the human family are greater than ever, bcause, through their own efforts, they are now beginning to play their full part in public life. We know so much more about what can

In October The Queen, visibly upset, meets survivors
from the Aberfan disaster. The small mining village in
south Wales lost 116 children and twenty-eight adults,
killed in a landslide of mining debris.

be achieved; we know that the tyranny of ignorance can be broken; we know the rules of health and how to protect children from disease.

We know all these things are important in our own homes, but it needs a very active concern by women everywhere if this knowledge is to be used where it is most needed. I am glad that in all countries of the Commonwealth women are more and more able to use it.

I am sure the custom of giving presents at Christmas will never die out, but I hope it will never overshadow the far more important presents we can give for the benefit of the future of the world. People of goodwill everywhere are working to build a world that will be a happier and more peaceful place in which to live. Let our prayers be for a personal strength and conviction to play our own small part to bring that day nearer. God be with you, and a very happy Christmas to you all.

The Queen presents the captain of England's football team, Bobby Moore with the Jules Rimet trophy after his team's memorable 4-2 victory over Germany in the 1966 World Cup.

# 1967

*In 1967 Canada celebrated the centenary of its Confederation, and The Queen and Prince Philip spent five weeks touring the country to mark the anniversary. In the same year The Queen knighted Sir Francis Chichester, the first man to sail solo around the world in his boat* Gipsy Moth IV. *The Queen's Christmas Broadcast for the year came from Buckingham Palace, and was shown in colour for the first time.*

Every once in a while an event occurs which seems to mark a milestone in history. For the Commonwealth, such an event was Canada's centenary this year. A hundred years ago the confederation of the provinces of Canada laid the foundations for the country's subsequent development. Once a land of pioneers largely dependent on agriculture and raw materials, Canada has become also one of the leading industrial nations of the world.

Prince Philip and I went to Ottawa for the Centenary celebrations and it was a most moving occasion. Canada has every reason to feel proud of her achievements in the last hundred years.

Confederation as a formal act could have achieved little by itself. Only the determined will of a great variety of individuals and groups to co-operate for the greater national interest could have breathed life into the creation of the Fathers of Confederation.

The future of Canada as a great and prosperous country depends just as much on the will of the present generation to work together. It is for them to continue and expand the process of development which began with such high hopes one hundred years ago.

Nothing has demonstrated this more forcefully than Expo '67, the remarkable international exhibition staged with such dramatic effect on a series of man-made islands in the St. Lawrence River. The theme of Expo was 'Man in his World', and the lasting impression which I took away with me from Canada's Centennial and Expo '67 is the degree of unity in outlook among the diverse nations, creeds and races of the world. The Commonwealth is a system which is in a constant process of change and development. This was brought home to me vividly when I revisited Malta only a month ago. When I first went to the islands, they were a colony and my husband was serving with the Mediterranean Fleet. Today Malta is independent, with the Crown occupying the same position as it does in the other self-governing countries

*The future of Canada as a great and prosperous country depends just as much on the will of the present generation to work together.*

of which I am Queen. This is the opening of a new and challenging chapter for the people of Malta and they are entering it with determination and enthusiasm.

Great national events can stir the imagination, but so can individual actions. Few people can have attracted so much universal attention as Sir Francis Chichester during his epic journey in *Gipsy Moth*. I am sure that the reason his great feat of seamanship so warmed our hearts was that we recognised in his enterprise and courage the very qualities which have played such a large part in British history and which we in these islands need just as much today and for the future.

Let there be no doubt that Britain is faced with formidable problems, but let there also be no doubt she will overcome them. Determined and well-directed effort by a people who for centuries have given ample evidence of their resources of character and initiative, must bring its reward.

I am glad to say that contacts at all levels between Commonwealth countries continue to grow, and I have been delighted to welcome Commonwealth prime ministers and leaders in various walks of life. Among the people who attract the greatest attention are visiting sportsmen and athletes. Cricket teams from India and Pakistan braved the vagaries of the English summer, and the redoubtable All Blacks from New Zealand have made a solid impact on British rugby footballers. Kenya sent us her great runner Kipchoge Keino. I hope many more sportsmen from Africa will take part in competitions and will establish new contacts between Africa and the rest of the world.

I have myself made many visits to other Commonwealth and overseas countries and every one was a journey of discovery. I am therefore particularly pleased that is it possible for so many young people and students to enjoy the experience of travel, to give service and to make new friends abroad.

My two elder children came back from the Commonwealth Games in Jamaica enchanted with the adventure, the kindness of the people, and the opportunity to meet so many athletes from every part of the Commonwealth. For my son this came at the end of a period in Australia, which he would not have missed for anything and where the exciting challenges and opportunities deeply impressed him.

In October this year, I took my son and daughter with me to the Opening of Parliament at Westminster. The Opening of Parliament is not just a ritual. It should remind us that Parliament symbolises the nation and the national interest. It should also remind us that we believe in government by consent and that our system can only work if we all want it to work and feel that we have some part in it. Democratic government is a tradition we all share and which is the ideal of all the members of our association of nations.

Modern communications make it possible for me to talk to you in your homes and to wish you a merry Christmas and a very happy New Year. These techniques of radio and television are modern, but the Christmas message is timeless. You may have heard it very often but in the end, no matter what scientific progress we make, the message will count for nothing unless we can achieve real peace and encourage genuine goodwill between individual people and the nations of the world.

Every Christmas I am sustained and encouraged by the happiness and sense of unity which comes from seeing all the members of my family together.

Enjoying the Canadian sunshine from their open-topped Lincoln Continental, The Queen and Prince Philip wave to crowds of well wishers, who greeted them at every stage of their state visit in 1967.

# 1968

*The Queen's Christmas Broadcast for 1968 — the year in which Civil Rights leader Martin Luther King was shot dead in Memphis — took the theme of the brotherhood of man. It was filmed in Buckingham Palace.*

Christmas is a Christian festival which celebrates the birth of the Prince of Peace. At times it is almost hidden by the merry making and tinsel, but the essential message of Christmas is still that we all belong to the great brotherhood of man.

This idea is not limited to the Christian faith. Philosophers and prophets have concluded that peace is better than war, love is better than hate and that mankind can only find progress in friendship and co-operation. Many ideas are being questioned today, but these great truths will continue to shine out as the light of hope in the darkness of intolerance and inhumanity.

The words 'the brotherhood of man' have a splendid ring about them, but the idea may seem too remote to have any practical meaning in this hard and bustling age. Indeed it means nothing at all unless the brotherhood, starting with individuals, can reconcile rival communities, conflicting religions, differing races and the divided and prejudiced nations of the world. If we truly believe that the brotherhood of man has a value for the world's future, then we should seek to support those international organisations which foster understanding between people and between nations.

The British people together have achieved great things in the past and have overcome many dangers, but we cannot make further progress if we resurrect ancient squabbles. The nations belonging to the Commonwealth have in their hands a well-tried framework for mutual help and co-operation. It would be short-sighted to waste this modest step towards brotherhood because we are too busy with the dissensions of the moment.

Every individual and every nation have problems, so there is all the more reason for us to do our utmost to show our concern for others. Rich or poor, we all depend upon the work and skill of individual men and women, particularly those in industry and production who are the creators of wealth and prosperity. We depend on new knowledge, invention and innovation, practical improvements and developments, all of which offer us a better life.

Yet we should not be obsessed by material problems. We must also be sure that we remain spiritually alive. Everything we do now is helping to shape the world in which our children are going to live. Our young people need all the help and opportunities we can give them to prepare them for the responsibilities which they will soon have to carry.

Today I have spoken of 'the brotherhood of man' and the hope it holds out for the world. This should not remain a vague thought nor an abstract idea. Each of us can put it into practice by treating one another with kindness and consideration at all times and in spite of every kind of provocation. Christmas is the festival of peace. It is God's will that it should be our constant endeavour to establish 'Peace on earth, goodwill towards men'. I hope you all have a very happy Christmas and every good fortune in the New Year.

The Queen Mother, the Duke of Beaufort and The Queen at an exciting moment during the Badminton Horse Trials in Gloucester in April.

# 1969

*For the only time in The Queen's reign to date, there was no Christmas Broadcast in
1969. This was because a special documentary film - 'Royal Family' - had been
made during the summer in connection with the Investiture of The Prince of Wales
The Queen issued a written message instead.*

I have received a great number of kind letters and messages of regard and concern about this year's break with the usual broadcast at Christmas and I want you all to know that my good wishes are no less warm and personal because they come to you in a different form.

In a short time the 1960s will be over but not out of our memories. Historians will record them as the decade in which men first reached out beyond our own planet and set foot on the moon, but each one of us will have our own special triumphs or tragedies to look back on.

My own thoughts are with my older children who are entering the service of the people of this country and the Commonwealth. It is a great satisfaction and comfort to me and my husband to know that they have won a place in your affections.

We are all looking forward to our visit to Australia and New Zealand for the Cook bi-centenary celebrations, and also to Fiji and Tonga. Later next year we hope to see something of the fascinating development of Northern Canada.

It is only natural that we should all be dazzled and impressed by the triumphs of technology, but Christmas is a festival of the spirit. At this time our concern is particularly for the lonely, the sick and the elderly. I hope they will all feel the warmth and comfort of companionship and that all of you will enjoy a very happy Christmas with your families and friends. God bless you all.

*Top:* Cameras were allowed unprecedented access to the royals for a year, however, while *Royal Family* was aired once on the BBC and again on ITV, the film was considered so intrusive that it has not been shown since ; *Above:* The Queen crowns Prince Charles as Prince of Wales during the televised investiture ceremony at Caernarvon Castle, Wales on 1 July.

# 1970

*The year 1970 marked the 200th anniversary of the voyage of Captain Cook 'discovering' Australia. The Queen's Christmas Broadcast that year recounted some of the trips made by The Queen earlier in the year. It included film shot in Australia, New Zealand and Canada.*

Every year we are reminded that Christmas is a family festival; a time for reunion and a meeting point for the generations. This year I am thinking of rather a special family — a family of nations — as I recall fascinating journeys to opposite ends of the world. During the course of these visits we met and talked with a great number of people in every sort of occupation, and living in every kind of community and climate. Yet in all this diversity they had one thing in common: they were all members of the Commonwealth family.

Early this year we went to Fiji, Tonga, New Zealand and Australia in Britannia. We were following the path taken in 1770 by that great English discoverer, Captain Cook. A little later in the year we were in Canada, still in the Commonwealth, visiting the North-west Territories and Manitoba for their centenaries. Among people who are so essentially New Zealanders, Canadians or Australians, it struck me again that so many of them still have affectionate and personal links with the British Isles. Wherever I went among people living in the busy industrial towns or on the stations and farms of the far outback, I met newcomers who reminded me that these links between our countries are renewed every year. In Canada we met some of the older inhabitants — the indigenous peoples — whose ancestors were there for generations before the Europeans came. And further north still live the Eskimos, some of the most interesting people that we met during our travels this year. They too belong to the Commonwealth family, this remarkable collection of friendly people of so many races.

Later in the year, representatives from forty-two different parts of the world gathered to attend the Commonwealth Games. There are many unpublicised meetings, but it is not often that the Commonwealth is able to get together for a great public ceremony. On this occasion it was sport that brought them to Scotland, and they came to compete and to enjoy themselves. We entertained them all in the garden of our home in Edinburgh, and I was very conscious that each of the athletes I met represented a country as different and interesting as those I had been able to visit during the year.

Never before has there been a group of independent nations linked in this way by their common history and continuing affection. Too often we hear about the Commonwealth only when there is bad news about one of its members, or when its usefulness or its very existence is questioned. Britain and other members responded generously after the terrible disaster in East Pakistan, but the fellowship of the Commonwealth does not exist only at such unhappy times.

The Queen and the Duke of Edinburgh share a smile during a state banquet.

Many of us here in Britain have relatives living in other Commonwealth countries, and there are many who were born overseas living here. Because it is Christmas we are probably thinking of them now. It is these personal contacts which mean so much. The strength of the Commonwealth lies in its history and the way people feel about it. All those years through which we have lived together have given us an exchange of people and ideas, which ensures that there is a continuing concern for each other. That, very simply, is the message of Christmas — learning to be concerned about one another; to treat your neighbour as you would like him to treat you; and to care about the future of all life on earth.

These matters of the spirit are more important and more lasting than simple material development. It is a hard lesson, but I think that we in the Commonwealth have perhaps begun to understand it. I wish you all a merry Christmas. God bless you all.

The Queen's younger sons, Princes Andrew (left)
and Edward appear in the Christmas Broadcast

# 1971

*The Queen's Christmas Broadcast focused on the theme of families.*
*The television version showed Prince Andrew and Prince Edward*
*looking at a family photograph album with their mother.*

Christmas is the time for families and for children, and it's also a time when we realise that another year is coming to an end. As the familiar pattern of Christmas and the New Year repeats itself, we may sometimes forget how much the world about us has been changing.

It was thirty nine years ago that my grandfather, King George V, gave the first of his Christmas Broadcasts. He spoke about a future which is now the past. Today it is our turn to think about the future.

Many of you who are listening are able, like me, to enjoy this Christmas with your families, and your children can enjoy the day as all children should. But tragically, there are many millions of others for whom this cannot be the same. Our thoughts and prayers should be for them.

Our children will be living in a world which our work and deeds have shaped for them. We cannot possibly tell what changes the next forty years will bring. We do know that we are passing on to our children the power to change their whole environment. But we also leave them with a set of values which they take from our lives and from our example. The decisions they take and the sort of world they pass on to their children could be just as much affected by those values as by all the technological wonders of the age.

The Christmas message is really one for all seasons and not just for one day of the year. If we can show this by our lives and by our example, then our contribution as parents will be just as important as any made by scientists and engineers. Perhaps we can then look for the real peace on earth, and the powers which men have harnessed will be used for the benefit of our fellow men.

I hope this Christmas Day is bringing to many of you peace and happiness, and for everyone the hope of this to come. May God bless you all.

# 1972 ~ 1981

## *A Time to* CELEBRATE

The Queen and Prince Phillip relaxing at Balmoral in 1975
with a corgi. Elizabeth has owned over thirty corgis during
her reign, after being given a corgi she named Susan
on her eighteenth birthday.

Elizabeth II celebrated her Silver Jubilee on her ascension to the throne throughout most of 1977. She kick-started her year by replying to an address from both Houses of Parliament on 4 May. Responding to such addresses is sometimes a tricky proposition as the reigning monarch must both remain politically neutral and yet explain their role in the government's plans for that session. On this occasion, it looked as though the Acts to allow referenda in Scotland and Wales for independence were now likely to be approved by Parliament so The Queen, slightly nervously, opined:

*They provide the background for the continuing and keen discussions of proposals for devolution to Scotland and Wales within the United Kingdom. But I cannot forget that I was crowned Queen of the United Kingdom of Great Britain and Northern Ireland. Perhaps this Jubilee is a time to remind ourselves of the benefits which union has conferred, at home and in our international dealings, on the inhabitants of all parts of this United Kingdom.*

The Queen broke all records that year, criss-crossing the nation accompanied by Prince Philip. She took in thirty six cities and counties, starting with Glasgow on 17 May. Huge crowds greeted her, especially – and for no particular reason – in Lancashire, where a record one million spectators turned out. There had already been a special church service day of commemoration on 6 February and a Jubilee weekend over four days was held in June to coincide with The Queen's 'official' birthday. This is always celebrated on the second Saturday of June – a tradition dating back to the time of King George II.

On 6 June, in the early evening, The Queen lit a bonfire beacon at Windsor Castle, which then connected to hundreds of beacons being lit up and down the land.

The next day, there were perhaps another million people who watched her procession to and from St Paul's Cathedral, for a service of thanksgiving that was attended by Prime Minister James Callaghan and former prime ministers Harold Macmillan, Lord Home, Sir Harold Wilson and Edward Heath.

Later, at a reception in the nearby Guildhall reception in the City of London, The Queen said:

*When I was twenty-one, I pledged my life to the service of our people and I asked God's help to make good that vow. Although that vow was made in my salad days, when I was green in judgement, I do not regret nor retract one word.*

There were street parties and fetes throughout the land, bringing our communities together with bunting, beer, Union Jacks, jollity and joy. The new tube line was named Jubilee in The Queen's honour, she attended the Wimbledon Championships as they celebrated their centenary (fortuitously seeing Virginia Wade win the final) and then, later in the year, she and her husband visited fourteen countries together, including Fiji, Tonga, New Zealand, Australia, Papua New Guinea and Canada.

But for all the relief of the Silver Jubilee and its celebrations, this was an uncomfortable decade, especially close to home in Northern Ireland with the outbreak of the 'Troubles'. British troops, sent into the province in 1969 to restore order after sectarian rioting, found themselves caught in the middle of renewed violent conflict between Protestant and Catholic populations, including the militant Catholic faction, known as the Provisional Irish Republican Army (IRA).

In January 1972, in what came to be called 'Bloody Sunday', UK 'paras' killed fourteen unarmed protesters. The response by the Provisional IRA was relentless, with a bombing campaign in Northern Ireland and England that continued throughout the 1970s, 1980s and 1990s, until the Good Friday Agreement was signed on 10 April 1998.

On the British mainland, deadly bombs were planted indiscriminately, targeting mainly military targets, including at the (then) Post Office Tower, Parliament, the Tower of London, also pubs in Guildford, Birmingham, and Coventry. Those murdered by the IRA included political activist Ross McWhirter, co-founder of Guinness Book of Records, who was shot and killed in north London by the IRA. More poignantly for the royal family, Lord Mountbatten, his 14-year-old grandson Nicholas Knatchbull and 15-year-old crew member Paul Maxwell were killed when Mountbatten's yacht was blown up while they were lobster-potting off the west coast of Ireland, close to the Northern Irish border.

The 1970s also marked the supposedly blackest day for the James Callaghan-led Labour Government, when the party lost a vote of no confidence (brought by Margaret Thatcher, Leader of the Opposition, on 28 March 1979) by just one: 311-310. Margaret Thatcher's win ultimately made her the first female prime minister, and ushered in a new look Conservative era.

Government was having a more difficult time of things across the Atlantic where the Republican President Richard Nixon resigned on 9 August 1974 after two years of relentless pressure; he was facing certain impeachment and removal from office and a potential prison sentence after continued attempts to cover up a break-in to the offices of the Democratic National Committee headquarters at the Watergate Office Building in Washington DC. The following year, the USA vetoed a UN resolution for an independent Palestinian state and the Vietnamese War ended with the humiliating withdrawal of US troops from Saigon.

The world of computing was moving from big-frame to hand-held with the Hewlett Packard pocket calculator in 1972, a snip at $399 .Then, almost without notice, a couple of geeks, Paul Allen and Bill Gates, gave birth to Microsoft in 1975. Not to be entirely outdone, the British and French co-funded and designed the supersonic airliner *Concorde,* which made its first commercial flight the following January, the same year that those unlikely 'twins' Steve Jobs and Steve Wozniak launched the Apple 1. A relatively unknown computer scientist called Tim Berners-Lee began work on ENQUIRE, which would eventually lead to him creating the world wide web in 1989.

There was also huge sadness in the UK throughout this decade. In 1974, 346 passengers died in a Turkish Airline crash just after take–off from Paris. The dead included local club rugby players from Bury St Edmunds and Bedford, who had just watched England draw 12-12 with France in the Five Nations. Later, in 1980, John Lennon's assassination in New York shocked the nation as well as the rest of the world.

There was better news when the sensational Opera House in Sydney was finally opened after a fourteen-year hiatus in its construction. And then, in mid-July 1981, Ian Botham and Bob Willis brought smiles to our faces with their stupendous performances in the Ashes, which England hosted and won 3-1. The following week, on 29 July, a 750-million worldwide television audience watched the wedding of Prince Charles to the 19-year-old Lady Diana Spencer in St Paul's Cathedral.

# 1972

*In 1972 The Queen and Prince Philip celebrated twenty-five years of marriage, and The Queen's Christmas Broadcast that year included scenes from the celebration. The year also saw terrible violence in Northern Ireland, and preparations for Britain to join the European Economic Community. The Queen refers to both these news stories in her speech.*

My whole family has been deeply touched by the affection you have shown to us when we celebrated our Silver Wedding, and we are especially grateful to the many thousands who have written to us and sent us messages and presents. One of the great Christian ideals is a happy and lasting marriage between man and wife, but no marriage can hope to succeed without a deliberate effort to be tolerant and understanding. This doesn't come easily to individuals and it certainly doesn't come naturally to communities or nations.

We know only too well that a selfish insistence upon our rights and our own point of view leads to disaster. We all ought to know by now that a civilised and peaceful existence is only possible when people make the effort to understand each other. Looking at the world, one might be forgiven for believing that many people have never heard of this simple idea. Every day there are reports of violence, lawlessness, and the disregard for human life. Most of this is excused on purely selfish grounds. I know there are millions of kindly people throughout the world who are saddened with me for all those who suffer from these outrages.

In the United Kingdom we have our own particular sorrows in Northern Ireland and I want to send a special message of sympathy to all those men, women and children who have suffered and endured so much. But there is a light in this tragic situation. The people are steadfastly carrying on their ordinary business in their factories and places of work.

Voluntary workers, both in and out of uniform, have struggled to keep humanity and common sense alive. The social services have done their job magnificently. The forces of law and order continue their thankless task with the utmost fortitude in the face of appalling provocation. We must admire them greatly for their patience and restraint. I ask you all to join me in praying that the hearts and minds of everyone in that troubled Province may be touched with the spirit of Christmas and the message of brotherhood, peace and goodwill. May tolerance and understanding release the people from terror and put gladness in the place of fear.

*No marriage can hope to succeed without a deliberate effort to be tolerant and understanding. This doesn't come easily to individuals and it certainly doesn't come naturally to communities or nations.*

On 14 November, Princess Anne married Captain Mark Philips at Westminster Abbey. Her nine-year-old brother Prince Edward was pageboy, and the bride's young cousin, Princess Margaret's daughter Lady Sarah Armstrong-Jones was bridesmaid.

*Previous page*, the Queen and The Duke of Edinburgh walking on the Balmoral Estate, Scotland in September 1972.

But I am speaking today to all the peoples of the Commonwealth. In this unique organisation, we are fortunate in having endless opportunities for co-operation. Through its informal structure we have created a web of relationships between peoples of many races and creeds and now between a great number of sovereign independent states.

I have visited almost all of the thirty-two independent Commonwealth countries, and we are looking forward to going back to Canada and Australia next year. I know from this personal experience how much the Commonwealth is valued by its members.

Britain is about to join her neighbours in the European Community and you may well ask how this will affect the Commonwealth. The new links with Europe will not replace those with the Commonwealth. They cannot alter our historical and personal attachments with kinsmen and friends overseas. Old friends will not be lost; Britain will take her Commonwealth links into Europe with her.

Christmas is above all a time of new life. A time to look hopefully ahead to a future when the problems which face the world today will be seen in their true perspective. I leave with you the old message, 'On earth peace; goodwill toward men'. No one has ever offered a better formula and I hope that its simple truth may yet take hold of the imagination of all mankind.

# 1973

*On 14 November Princess Anne married Captain Mark Phillips at Westminster*
*Abbey in a televised ceremony with an estimated audience of 100 million. The Queen's*
*Christmas Broadcast included footage shot at Buckingham Palace on the wedding day.*

It is now twenty-one years since I first broadcast a Christmas Message to the Commonwealth. Then our two elder children were only four and two. Now, our daughter joins us for Christmas with her husband and we are celebrating the festival this year with the memories of their wedding very much in our minds.

We are constantly being told that we live in a changing world and that we need to adapt to changing conditions. But this is only part of the truth and I am sure that all parents seeing their children getting married are reminded of the continuity of human life. That is why, I think, that at weddings all friends and relations, and even complete strangers, can stop worrying for a moment and share in the happiness of the couple who are getting married.

I am glad that my daughter's wedding gave such pleasure to so many people just at a time when the world was facing very serious problems. People all over the world watched the wedding on television, but there were still many in London on the day, and their warmth and enthusiasm ensured it was an occasion my family will never forget.

Earlier this year, I went to Canada for a different sort of 'family occasion'. This was the meeting of Commonwealth Heads of Government, and here, I was reminded of the importance of human relationships in world affairs, and how membership of the Commonwealth has a subtle influence on the relationships between its leaders.

I was impressed by the spirit that brought together so many leaders from such different countries, and enabled them to discuss constructively matters that concern us all as friends. Those of you who are surrounded by friends – or, of course, who are members of a happy family – know this makes life much easier.

Everything — the good and the bad — can be shared, but it is too easy for us to forget those who are not so fortunate. However, there are many people of all ages who go out to help the old and the lonely, the sick and the handicapped. I am sure that, in so doing, they find the real happiness that comes from serving and thinking of others.

I believe that Christmas should remind us that the qualities of the human spirit are more important than material gain. Christ taught love and charity and that we should show humanity and compassion at all times and in all situations.

A lack of humanity and compassion can be very destructive – how easily this causes diversions within nations and between nations. We should remember instead how much we have in common and resolve to give expression to the best of our human qualities, not only at Christmas, but right through the year.

In this Christmas spirit let us greet all our fellow men and join together in this festival of tolerance and companionship. I wish you all a very happy Christmas.

During a royal visit to Alberta and Saskatchewan in July 1973, The Queen inspects a line of Royal Canadian Mounted Police (The Mounties) as part of the force's centennial celebrations.

# 1974

*In her Christmas Broadcast The Queen alluded to the many problems around the world, including the continuing violence in Northern Ireland and the Middle East. She also reminded us that we need to work together to solve conflict.*

There can be few people in any country of the Commonwealth who are not anxious about what is happening in their own countries or in the rest of the world at this time. We have never been short of problems, but in the last year everything seems to have happened at once. There have been floods and drought and famine: there have been outbreaks of senseless violence. And on top of it all the cost of living continues to rise — everywhere. Here in Britain, from where so many people of the Commonwealth came, we hear a great deal about our troubles, about discord and dissension and about the uncertainty of our future. Perhaps we make too much of what is wrong and too little of what is right. The trouble with gloom is that it feeds upon itself and depression causes more depression. There are indeed real dangers and there are real fears and we will never overcome them if we turn against each other with angry accusations.

We may hold different points of view but it is in times of stress and difficulty that we most need to remember that we have much more in common than there is dividing us. We have the lessons of history to show that the British people have survived many a desperate situation when they acted together.

People in a crowd may seem oblivious of each other. Yet if you look at your neighbours you will see other people with worries and difficulties probably greater than your own. It is time to recognise that in the end we all depend upon each other and that we are therefore responsible for each other.

Fortunately over the centuries we have devised a way of sharing this responsibility, a uniquely effective system for bringing progress out of conflict. We have developed Parliamentary Government by which the rights and freedom of the people are maintained. It allows change to take place temperately and without violence. And when time demands, it can reflect and give a voice to the determination and resolve of the Nation. This system, this product of British genius, has been successfully exported to the world wide Commonwealth. This year I have opened Parliament four times: in New Zealand, in Australia, and twice the Mother of Parliaments in Westminster. I suspect this may be a record, but what impressed me was that the system itself flourishes thousands of miles away and this alone should give us confidence.

The Queen at an inspection of the Yeoman of the Guard, a corp of Royal Bodyguards at Buckingham Palace. They, and the Yeoman Warders of HM Tower of London, a separate corps, are popularly known as 'beefeaters', possibly derived from the large meat ration they once enjoyed as the monarch's personal bodyguards.

You may be asking what can we do personally to make things better? I believe the Christmas message provides the best clue. Goodwill is better than resentment, tolerance is better than revenge, compassion is better than anger, above all a lively concern for the interests of others as well as our own. In times of doubt and anxiety the attitudes people show in their daily lives, in their homes, and in their work, are of supreme importance. It is by acting in this spirit that every man, woman and child can help and 'make a difference'.

In Britain I am sure it could make all the difference. We are an inventive and tenacious people and the comradeship of adversity brings out the best in us. And we have great resources, not just those of character but in our industry and trade, in our farms and in the seas around our shores.

My message today is one of encouragement and hope. Christmas on this side of the equator comes at the darkest time of the year: but we can look forward hopefully to lengthening days and the returning sun. The first Christmas came at a time that was dark and threatening, but from it came the light of the world. I wish you all a happy Christmas.

# 1975

*The Queen's Christmas Broadcast in 1975 was broadcast from the gardens of Buckingham Palace; the first time the message had been recorded out of doors. It was a year of record inflation and unemployment in the UK and worldwide and The Queen referred to the challenges faced by many nations.*

Every year I have this special opportunity of wishing you a happy Christmas. I like to think I am speaking to each child who can see or hear me, each woman, each man in every country of the Commonwealth.

Christmas is a festival which brings us together in small groups, a family group if we are lucky. Today we are not just nameless people in a crowd. We meet as friends who are glad to be together and who care about each other's happiness. Nowadays this is a precious experience. So much of the time we feel that our lives are dominated by great impersonal forces beyond our control, the scale of things and organisations seems to get bigger and more inhuman.

We are horrified by brutal and senseless violence, and above all the whole fabric of our lives is threatened by inflation, the frightening sickness of the world today. Then Christmas comes, and once again we are reminded that people matter, and it is our relationship with one another that is most important.

For most of us – I wish it could be for everyone – this is a holiday, and I think it's worth reminding ourselves why. We are celebrating a birthday – the birthday of a child born nearly 2,000 years ago, who grew up and lived for only about 3 years.

That one person, by his example and by his revelation of the good which is in us all, has made an enormous difference to the lives of people who have come to understand his teaching. His simple message of love has been turning the world upside down ever since. He showed that what people are and what they do, does matter and does make all the difference.

He commanded us to love our neighbours as we love ourselves, but what exactly is meant by 'loving ourselves'? I believe it means trying to make the most of the abilities we have been given, it means caring for our talents. It is a matter of making the best of ourselves, not just doing the best for ourselves.

*If you throw a stone into a pool, the ripples go on spreading outwards. A big stone can change the whole pattern of the water.*

We are all different, but each of us has his own best to offer. The responsibility for the way we live life with all its challenges, sadness and joy is ours alone. If we do this well, it will also be good for our neighbours.

If you throw a stone into a pool, the ripples go on spreading outwards. A big stone can cause waves, but even the smallest pebble changes the whole pattern of the water. Our daily actions are like those ripples, each one makes a difference, even the smallest.

It does matter therefore what each individual does each day. Kindness, sympathy, resolution, and courteous behaviour are infectious. Acts of courage and self-sacrifice, like those of the people who refuse to be terrorised by kidnappers or hijackers, or who defuse bombs, are an inspiration to others.

And the combined effect can be enormous. If enough grains of sand are dropped into one side of a pair of scales they will, in the end, tip it against a lump of lead. We may feel powerless alone but the joint efforts of individuals can defeat the evils of our time. Together they can create a stable, free and considerate society.

Like those grains of sand, they can tip the balance. So take heart from the Christmas message and be happy.

During her first and only trip to Japan in 1976, The Queen and Prince Philip stroll in the grounds of Kyoto Palace on the island on Honshu Island, pausing to feed golden carp accompanied by their host, Emperor Hirohito.

# 1976

*In 1976 The Queen and Prince Philip undertook a State Visit to the United States, to mark America's bicentenary. The royal couple were welcomed by President Ford, and The Queen presented a new Liberty Bell to Philadelphia. That visit formed the theme of The Queen's Christmas Broadcast in 1976.*

Christmas is a time for reconciliation. A time not only for families and friends to come together but also for differences to be forgotten. In 1976 I was reminded of the good that can flow from a friendship that is mended. Two hundred years ago the representatives of the thirteen British Colonies in North America signed the Declaration of Independence in Philadelphia.

This year we went to America to join in their bicentennial celebrations. Who would have thought 200 years ago that a descendent of King George III could have taken part in these celebrations? Yet that same King was among the first to recognise that old scores must be settled and differences reconciled, and the first United States Ambassador to Britain declared that he wanted 'the old good nature and the old good humour restored'. And restored they were. The United States was born in bitter conflict with Britain but we didn't remain enemies for long. From our reconciliation came incalculable benefits to mankind and a partnership which, together with many countries of the Commonwealth, was proved in two World Wars and ensured that the light of liberty was not extinguished.

King George III never saw the Colonies he lost. My father, King George VI, was the first British Sovereign to see the famous skyline of Manhattan and to visit the rich and vibrant country that lies beyond it. Wherever we went the welcome was the same, all the way to Boston, where the first shots in the war between Britain and America were fired.

Reconciliation, like the one that followed the American War of Independence, is the product of reason, tolerance and love, and I think that Christmas is a good time to reflect on it. It is easy enough to see where reconciliation is needed and where it would heal and purify, obviously in national and international affairs, but also in homes and families. It is not something that is easy to achieve. But things that are worthwhile seldom are, so it is encouraging to know that there are many people trying to achieve it.

A few weeks ago, for instance, I met in my home a group of people who are working for better understanding between people of different colour, different faiths

and different philosophies — and who are trying to solve the very real problems of community relations. Another shining example is the peace movement in Northern Ireland. Here Roman Catholics and Protestants have joined together in a crusade of reconciliation to bring peace to the Province.

Next year is a rather special one for me and I would like my Silver Jubilee year also to become a special one for people who find themselves the victims of human conflict. The gift I would most value next year is that reconciliation should be found wherever it is needed. A reconciliation which would bring peace and security to families and neighbours at present suffering and torn apart. Remember that good spreads outwards and every little does help. Mighty things from small beginnings grow as indeed they grew from the small child of Bethlehem.

I believe there is another thought from which we can draw encouragement. If there is reconciliation – if we can get the climate right – the good effects will flow much more quickly than most people would believe possible. Those who know the desert know also how quickly it can flower when the rains come. But who in Britain who saw the parched earth and empty reservoirs last summer would have believed that the grass would grow so strong, so green and so soon when the drought ended? When the conflict stops, peace can blossom just as quickly. I wish you all a very happy Christmas and may the New Year bring reconciliation between all people.

American President Gerald Ford leads The Queen onto the dance floor during a ball at the White House, Washington, part of the 1976 bicentennial celebrations of the Declaration of Independence.

# 4 MAY 1977
# THE SILVER JUBILEE

*During celebrations of her twenty-five years on the throne, The Queen replied to an address from both Houses of Parliament. She reflected on her reign and also referred, obliquely, to the challenge of devolution for Scotland and Wales.*

I am deeply grateful for your Loyal Addresses and for the kind and generous words in which the Lord Chancellor and Mr. Speaker have expressed them. Thank you also for what you have said about my family and the service they have given over the years. You will understand that for me personally their support has been invaluable.

It is appropriate that I should come to Westminster at the start of the Jubilee celebrations in the United Kingdom. Here, in a meeting of Sovereign and Parliament, the essence of Constitutional Monarchy is reflected. It is a form of Government in which those who represent the main elements of the community can come together to reconcile conflicting interests and to strive for the hopes and aims we all share. It has adapted itself to the changes in our own society and in international relationships, yet it has remained true to its essential role. It has provided the fabric of good order in society and has been the guardian of the liberties of individual citizens.

These 25 years have seen much change for Britain. By virtue of tolerance and understanding, the Empire has evolved into a Commonwealth of thirty six Independent Nations spanning the five Continents. No longer an Imperial Power, we have been coming to terms with what this means for ourselves and for our relations with the rest of the world. We have forged new links with other countries and in joining the European Economic Communities we have taken what is perhaps one of the most significant decisions during my reign.

At home there are greater opportunities for all sorts and conditions of men and women. Developments in science, technology and in medicine have improved the quality and comfort of life and, of course, there has also been television!

We in Government and Parliament have to accept the challenges which this progress imposes on us. And they are considerable. The problems of progress, the complexities of modern administration, the feeling that Metropolitan Government is too remote from the lives of ordinary men and women, these among other things have helped to revive an awareness of historic national identities in these Islands. They provide the background for the continuing and keen discussion of proposals for devolution to Scotland and Wales within the United Kingdom.

I number Kings and Queens of England and of Scotland, and Princes of Wales among my ancestors and so I can readily understand these aspirations. But I cannot forget that I was crowned Queen of the United Kingdom of Great Britain and Northern Ireland. Perhaps this Jubilee is a time to remind ourselves of the benefits which union has conferred, at home and in our international dealings, on the inhabitants of all parts of this United Kingdom.

A Jubilee is also a time to look forward! We should certainly do this with determination and I believe we can also do so with hope. We have so many advantages, the basic stability of our institutions, our traditions of public service and concern for others, our family life and, above all, the freedom which you and your predecessors in Parliament have, through the ages, so fearlessly upheld.

My Lords, Members of the House of Commons. For me the twenty fifth anniversary of my Accession is a moving occasion. It is also, I hope, for all of us a joyous one. May it also be a time in which we can all draw closer together.

Thank you again! I begin these celebrations much encouraged by your good wishes and expressions of loyalty.

*Overleaf,* images from the Silver Jubilee celebrations:
*Left:* The Queen at a Royal Gala performance at Covent Garden;
*above*: After a lunch at Guildhall, The Queen and Prince Philip return to Buckingham Palace;

*below:* The Queen greets crowds of well wishers in Scotland, as part of her Silver Jubilee tour.

# 1977

*This was the year of The Queen's Silver Jubilee, and in addition to addressing Parliament in May at the start of the celebrations, The Queen used her Christmas Broadcast to recall highlights what was a very happy year for her.*

I shall never forget the scene outside Buckingham Palace on Jubilee Day. The cheerful crowd was symbolic of the hundreds of thousands of people who greeted us wherever we went in this Jubilee Year — in twelve Commonwealth countries and thirty-six counties in the United Kingdom.

But I believe it also revealed to the world that we can be a united people. It showed that all the artificial barriers which divide man from man and family from family can be broken down. The street parties and village fêtes, the presents, the flowers from the children, the mile upon mile of decorated streets and houses; these things suggest that the real value and pleasure of the celebration was that we all shared in it together.

Last Christmas I said that my wish for 1977 was that it should be a year of reconciliation. You have shown by the way in which you have celebrated the Jubilee that this was not an impossible dream. Thank you all for your response.

Nowhere is reconciliation more desperately needed than in Northern Ireland. That is why I was particularly pleased to go there. No one dared to promise an early end to the troubles but there is no doubt that people of goodwill in Northern Ireland were greatly heartened by the chance they had to share the celebrations with the rest of the nation and Commonwealth.

Many people in all parts of the world have demonstrated this goodwill in a practical way by giving to the Silver Jubilee Appeal. The results of their kindness will be appreciated by young people — and by those they are able to help — for many years to come.

The great resurgence of community spirit that has marked the celebrations has shown the value of the Christian ideal of loving our neighbours. If we can keep this spirit alive, life will become better for all of us.

The Jubilee celebrations in London started with a Service of Thanksgiving in St. Paul's Cathedral. To me this was a thanksgiving for all the good things for which our Commonwealth stands – the comradeship and co-operation it inspires and the friendship and tolerance it encourages. These are the qualities needed by all mankind.

The evening before the Service I lit one small flame at Windsor and a chain of bonfires spread throughout Britain and on across the world to New Zealand and Australia. My hope this Christmas is that the Christian spirit of reconciliation may burn as strongly in our hearts during the coming year. God bless you and a very happy Christmas to you all.

The Queen meets some of the Maori people on her royal tour of New Zealand.

# 1978

*The Queen's Christmas Message in 1978 took the theme of the future. The broadcast included footage of The Queen with her new grandson, Peter Phillips, and Princess Anne, as well as recordings of earlier broadcasts going back to King George V.*

At Christmas, we look back nearly 2000 years to an event that was to bring new hope and new confidence to all subsequent generations. The birth of Christ gave us faith in the future and as I read through some earlier Christmas Broadcasts, I was struck by the way that this same idea – faith in the future – kept recurring.

My grandfather, King George V, started the tradition of the Christmas Day Broadcasts back in 1932. As he spoke from his study at Sandringham, the 'wireless' – as we used to call it – made it possible for millions of people throughout the world to hear the voice of the Sovereign for the first time. And in that first broadcast, they heard him talk about the future – as he saw in 1932.

[The Broadcast then featured a recording of the voice of King George V from 1932]

> *It may be that our future will lay upon us more than one stern test. Our past will have taught us how to meet it unshaken. For the present, the work to which we are all equally bound is to arrive at a reasoned tranquillity within our borders; to regain prosperity without self-seeking; and to carry with us those whom the burden of past years has disheartened or overborne.*
>
> VOICE OF KING GEORGE VI (1932)

My father, King George VI, developed this theme of optimism and hope, even during the most difficult years of his reign.On Christmas Day 1939, just after the outbreak of the Second World War, he spoke the words that many of you listening today will remember well.

> *I feel that we may all find a message of encouragement in the lines which, in my closing words, I would like to say to you:- "I said to the man who stood at the Gate of the Year, "Give me a light that I may tread safely into the unknown. And he replied, "Go out into the darkness and put your hand into the Hand of God. That shall be to you better than light and safer than a known way".*
>
> VOICE OF KING GEORGE VI (1939)

At the end of the war in Europe, there was rejoicing everywhere, although beneath it all the problems of the world were only too evident. But on Christmas Day 1945, my father expressed undiminished hope and trust in the future.

> *Have faith in life at its best and bring to it your courage, your hopes and your sense of humour. For merriment is the birthright of the young. But we can all keep it in our hearts as life goes on, if we hold fast by the spirit that refuses to admit defeat; by the faith that never falters; by the hope that cannot be quenched. Let us have no fear of the future but think of it as opportunity and adventure.*
>
> KING GEORGE VI (1945)

The optimism of that Christmas message is timeless. When it first fell to me to carry on the tradition that my grandfather and father had developed, I reaffirmed what I knew had been their deeply held beliefs in the future, beliefs which I myself share. This is what I said on Christmas Day 1952:

> *Many grave problems and difficulties confront us all, but with a new faith in the old and splendid beliefs given us by our forefathers and the strength to venture beyond the safeties of the past, I know we shall be worthy of our duty.*

By 1957 television was a feature of most homes and for the first time the broadcast was televised. That year I spoke on Christmas Day of the qualities needed to sustain our faith in the future.

> *Today we need a special kind of courage but not the kind needed in battle but a kind which makes us stand up for everything that we know is right, everything that is true and honest. We need the kind of courage that can withstand the subtle corruption of the cynics so that we can show the world that we are not afraid of the future.*

You have heard three generations talking about the future. My grandfather couldn't have known what was in store for his grandchildren; yet his faith in the future gave him a quiet confidence that the stern tests would be overcome. And so it has proved. My father watched his grandchildren take their first steps and he knew that all the sacrifices and anxiety of the dark days of the War had been worthwhile.

Now it is our turn to work for a future which our grandchildren will step into one day. We cannot be certain what lies ahead for them but we should know enough to put them on the right path. We can do this if we have the good sense to learn from the experience of those who have gone before us and to hold on to all the good that has been handed down to us in trust.Look around at your families as you are gathered together for Christmas. Look at the younger ones – they are the future and just as we were helped to understand and to appreciate the values of a civilised community, it is now our responsibility to help them to do the same.

The Queen and Prince Philip, with Prince Charles seated to The Queen's right, during the State Opening of Parliament in October 1978.

We must not let the difficulties of the present or the uncertainties of the future cause us to lose faith. You remember the saying 'the optimist proclaims that we live in the best of all possible worlds, and the pessimist fears that this is true'. It is far from easy to be cheerful and constructive when things around us suggest the opposite; but to give up the effort would mean, as it were, to switch off hope for a better tomorrow. Even if the problems seem overwhelming, there is always room for optimism. Every problem presents us with the opportunity both to find an answer for ourselves and to help others.

The context of the lives of the next generation is being set, here and now, not so much by the legacy of science or wealth or political structure that we shall leave behind us, but by the example of our attitudes and behaviour to one another and by trying to show unselfish, loving and creative concern for those less fortunate than ourselves.

Christians have the compelling example of the life and teaching of Christ and, for myself, I would like nothing more than that my grandchildren should hold dear his ideals which have helped and inspired so many previous generations.I wish you all, together with your children and grandchildren, a very happy Christmas.

# 1979

*This was the Year of the Child, and The Queen's Christmas Broadcast addressed the theme of children and young people. It was a year that saw hundreds of thousands of refugees fleeing Cambodia following the disastrous rule of the Khmer Rouge.*

Every two years the Heads of Government of the Commonwealth countries meet together to discuss matters of mutual interest. This year they met in Africa and once again the meeting demonstrated the great value of personal contact and the desire of all the leaders to settle their differences in the friendly spirit of a family gathering. All thirty-nine full members of the Commonwealth were represented there and, as always on these occasions, I greatly valued the opportunity of talks with them.

One of the main objectives of Heads of Government is to make the world a better place for the next generation. 1979 has been the International Year of the Child and the Commonwealth has always stressed the importance of our young people: but this year people all over the world have been asked to give particular thought to the special needs of sick and handicapped children, to the hungry and homeless and to those in trouble or distress wherever they may be found.

It is an unhappy coincidence that political and economic forces have made this an exceptionally difficult and tragic year for many families and children in several parts of the world — but particularly in South East Asia. The situation has created a desperately serious challenge and I am glad to know that so many people of the Commonwealth have responded with wonderful generosity and kindness. It seems that the greater the needs of children, the more people everywhere rise to the occasion.

My daughter, as President of the Save the Children Fund, saw some of these volunteers looking after refugee children in the Far East. Nowhere is the voluntary effort more active than in charities and organisations devoted to helping children to survive the hazards to which they have been subjected.

The Year of the Child has emphasised the value of this work, but we must not forget that every generation has to face the problems of childhood and the stresses of growing up, and, in due course, the responsibilities of parents and adults. If they are

Prime Minister Margaret Thatcher chats to The Queen during a
Commonwealth Conference held in Zambia in 1979.

The Queen and her daughter take her first grandchild, Princess Anne's son Peter Phillips, for a walk.

handicapped in themselves, or by their family or community, their problems are all the more difficult.

Children are born with a mixed package of emotions, talents and handicaps, but without knowledge or experience. As they grow up they have to learn to live with their parents and families; and they have to adjust to school, including the discovery of leisure activities and learning to handle their relationships with their contemporaries and with strangers.

Schools, charities and voluntary organisations and institutions can do a great deal to help, and I have admired their work in many parts of the world; but in the end each one of us has a primary and personal responsibility for our own children, for children entrusted to our care and for all the children in our own communities.

At Christmas we give presents to each other. Let us also stop to think whether we are making enough effort to pass on our experience of life to our children. Today we celebrate the birth of the child who transformed history and gave us a great faith. Jesus said: Suffer the little children to come unto me and forbid them not, or of such is the kingdom of God. I wish you all a very happy Christmas.

# 1980

*In August Queen Elizabeth, The Queen Mother, celebrated her eightieth birthday. In her Christmas Broadcast, The Queen reflected on the celebrations and addressed the theme of service in its many forms.*

I was glad that the celebrations of my mother's eightieth birthday last summer gave so much pleasure. I wonder whether you remember, during the Thanksgiving Service in St. Paul's, the congregation singing that wonderful hymn 'Immortal, Invisible, God only wise'.

> *Now give us we pray thee the Spirit of love,*
> *The gift of true wisdom that comes from above,*
> *The spirit of service that has naught of pride,*
> *The gift of true courage, and thee as our guide.*

Did you catch the words of that hymn?

> *The spirit of service that has naught of pride,*
> *The gift of true courage, and thee as our guide.*

The loyalty and affection, which so many people showed to my mother, reflected a feeling, expressed in many different ways, that she is a person who has given selfless service to the people of this country and of the Commonwealth.

As I go about the country and abroad I meet many people who, all in their own ways, are making a real contribution to their community. I come across examples of unselfish service in all walks of life and in many unexpected places.

Some people choose their occupation so that they can spend their lives in the service of their fellow citizens. We see doctors, nurses and hospital staff caring for the sick; those in the churches and religious communities; in central and local Government; in the armed services; in the police and in the courts and prisons; in industry and commerce.

It is the same urge to make a contribution that drives those seeking the highest standards in education or art, in music or architecture. Others find ways to give service in their spare time, through voluntary organisations or simply on their own

*The loyalty and affection, which so many people showed to my mother, reflected a feeling expressed in many different ways, that she is a person who has given selfless service to the people of this country and of the Commonwealth.*

individual initiative contributing in a thousand ways to all that is best in our society. It may be providing company for the old and housebound; help for the disabled; care for the deprived and those in trouble; concern for neighbours or encouragement for the young.

To all of you on this Christmas Day, whatever your conditions of work and life, easy or difficult; whether you feel that you are achieving something or whether you feel frustrated; I want to say a word of thanks.

And I include all those who don't realise that they deserve thanks and are content that what they do is unseen and unrewarded. The very act of living a decent and upright life is in itself a positive factor in maintaining civilised standards.

We face grave problems in the life of our country, but our predecessors, and many alive today, have faced far greater difficulties, both in peace and war, and have overcome them by courage and calm determination. They never lost hope and they never lacked confidence in themselves or in their children.

In difficult times we may be tempted to find excuses for self-indulgence and to wash our hands of responsibility. Christmas stands for the opposite. The Wise Men and the Shepherds remind us that it is not enough simply to do our jobs; we need to go out and look for opportunities to help those less fortunate than ourselves, even if that service demands sacrifice. It was their belief and confidence in God which inspired them to visit the stable and it is this unselfish will to serve that will see us through the difficulties we face.

We know that the world can never be free from conflict and pain, but Christmas also draws our attention to all that is hopeful and good in this changing world; it speaks of values and qualities that are true and permanent and it reminds us that the world we would like to see can only come from the goodness of the heart.

When you hear the bells ringing at Christmas, think of the lines written by Tennyson:

> *Ring out false pride in place and blood,*
> *The civic slander and the spite;*
> *Ring in the love of truth and right,*
> *Ring in the common love of good …*
>
> *Ring in the valiant man and free,*
> *The larger heart, the kindlier hand,*
> *Ring out the darkness of the land,*
> *Ring in the Christ that is to be.*

To all of you, wherever you may be, I wish happiness this Christmas.

# 1981

*The Queen's Christmas Broadcast in 1981 marked the International Year of Disabled People, a year in which the courage and needs of the disabled came to prominence. The broadcast was recorded on the terrace of Buckingham Palace, overlooking the garden.*

Last July we had the joy of seeing our eldest son married amid scenes of great happiness, which made 1981 a very special year for us. The wonderful response the wedding evoked was very moving.

Just before that there had been a very different scene here in the garden at Buckingham Palace when three and a half thousand disabled people, with their families, came to tea with us. And, with members of my family, I have just met some more disabled people who came here to receive special cars which will give them the mobility they so desperately need. We handed over the keys of the new cars and also talked to handicapped people who have had their cars for some time.

The International Year of Disabled People has performed a very real service by focusing our attention on their problems. We have all become more aware of them and I'm sure that many of you, like myself, have been impressed by the courage they show.

There are, of course, many aspects of courage. There is the physical courage shown in war. Chesterton described it as 'almost a contradiction in terms … a strong desire to live taking the form of a readiness to die'. It is sobering and inspiring to remember what man will do for an ideal in which he believes.

Bravery of this kind is shown in peace as well as in war. The armed forces and the police are showing it every day. So are the fire services, ambulance drivers, members of the public and even children – and the courage of the bomb disposal experts fills us with awe. All around us we see these acts of selflessness, people putting the life of someone else before their own.

Then there is perseverance, sticking to the job. This is how the disabled have learnt to cope with life, becoming better people in the process. Their courage in handling their difficulties and in many cases living an almost normal life, or making abnormal life normal, shows our own problems to be insignificant in comparison. It is not only the disabled who are showing day-to-day perseverance and courage. This Christmas we should remember especially: the people of Northern Ireland who are attempting to live ordinary lives in times of strain and conflict; the unemployed who are trying to maintain their self-respect without work and to care for their families; and those from other parts of the Commonwealth who have come to Britain to make new lives but have not yet found themselves fully accepted.

Perhaps the greatest contribution of the disabled is to give the inspiration and incentive to do more to help others. From this we can gain the strength to try to do that little bit extra, as individuals, as members of our families and as nations. We have seen in 1981 how many individuals have devoted themselves to trying to make life more tolerable for handicapped people, by giving loving care and by providing money and effort to improve facilities and to hasten research. There are 450 million disabled people in the world, but wonderful work is being done in the prevention and cure of disablement. Diseases like polio and measles can be controlled by a very cheap multiple vaccine. In the last twelve years the Royal Commonwealth Society for the Blind has restored sight to over one million Commonwealth citizens.

But throughout this century there have been great advances in the awakening of conscience and concern for our fellow human beings. Governments now regard it as their duty to try to protect their people, through social services, from the worst effects of illness, bereavement, joblessness and disability.

We are also trying to reach beyond a nation's responsibility for its own citizens. There is a wide disparity between the wealth of nations and I have found that there is a spirit of eagerness to redress this throughout the world.

I have spoken of courage in its different forms and of the effect a display of courage can have on the world in which we live. Ultimately, however, we accept in our hearts that most important of all is moral courage. As human beings we generally know what is right and how we should act and speak. But we are also very aware of how difficult it is to have the courage of our convictions.

Our Christian faith helps us to sustain those convictions. Christ not only revealed to us the truth in his teachings. He lived by what he believed and gave us the strength to try to do the same — and, finally, on the cross, he showed the supreme example of physical and moral courage.

That sacrifice was the dawn of Christianity and this is why at Christmas time we are inspired by the example of Christ as we celebrate his birth. A few weeks ago I was sent this poem:

> *When all your world is torn with grief and strife*
> *Think yet — when there seems nothing left to mend*
> *The frail and time-worn fabric of your life,*
> *The golden thread of courage has no end.*

So to you all I say – God bless you, and a very happy Christmas.

Newly-weds The Princess and Prince of Wales wave from the
famous Buckingham Palace balcony after their wedding at
St Paul's Cathedral, with the three youngest bridesmaids.

# 1982 ~ 1991

## *The* SPECIAL RELATIONSHIP

The Queen and Prince Philip in The Green Room, Windsor Castle
in November 1987, in one of a series of photographs to
commemorate their Golden Wedding Anniversary.

Prince Charles and Princess Diana welcomed their first son Prince William Arthur Philip Louis to the world on 21 June 1982 at St Mary's Hospital, Paddington. He immediately became the second heir to the throne. Two years later the royal couple welcomed their second child, Prince Henry (Harry) Charles Albert David who was born on 15 September 1984.

The early part of this decade was dominated by Prime Minister Thatcher taking the country to war with Argentina in 1982 to defend the British sovereignty of the Falkland Islands in the South Atlantic. Parliament had been recalled to debate the issues on 3 April 1982, the day after the Argentinian army invaded and occupied the islands. In one of his last speeches of note, in his role as Ulster Unionist Member of Parliament, Enoch Powell commanded the attention of the Chamber: *The Prime Minister, shortly after she came into office, received a sobriquet as the "Iron Lady".… In the next week or two this House, the nation and the Rt Honourable Lady will learn of what metal she is made of.*

The Queen followed this war more keenly than others as her son Prince Andrew was serving as a helicopter pilot at the time and was involved in multiple missions to defend the Falkland Islands.

Thatcher's brave decision to go to war, and our overwhelming success against the Argentinians (who surrendered after 74 days, returning the islands to British control) ensured her a landslide victory in the 1983 General Election against Michael Foot MP, the leader of the Labour Party. The Conservatives won by 397 seats to 209. It was hard to envision Labour ever winning again.

*Time* magazine's choice of Man of the Year 1982 was prescient and cool: it chose 'The Computer'. Ironically, that same year, Rich Skrenta, then a teenager, had also created the first computer virus. It was called the 'Elk Cloner' and it infested the Apple II. 'Virus' might soon become the 'Word of the Decade'. A year later, the Advanced Research Projects Agency Network (known as ARPANET), an arm of the US Defence Department initially created to link computers at government-funded institutions, migrated to a different system, which successfully connected computers globally, heralding the beginning of the modern internet.

The Provisional IRA made an audacious attempt to assassinate Prime Minister Thatcher and her Cabinet during the annual Conservative Party Conference, bombing the Grand Hotel in Brighton where they were staying on 12 October 1984. Although Thatcher and her Cabinet members all survived, five senior Conservative members were killed and a further thiry four were taken to hospital, some of whom were severely injured for life.

On 7 February 1991 the IRA tried for a second time to kill a Prime Minister – this time John Major and his Cabinet — by launching three home-made mortar-bombs in the heart of London. The would-be assassins parked a van at the junction of Horse Guards Avenue and Whitehall and took aim at Number 10 Downing Street, where the Cabinet was meeting to discuss the ongoing Gulf War. One of the shells, 4.5 feet long and weighing 140 pounds (60 kilograms) fell just short of the Cabinet Room, exploding in the Downing Street garden barely thirty feet away. No one was killed and injuries were slight. There were bomb attacks just over a week later at both London's Victoria and Paddington stations.

It was not all doom and gloom: the TV station Channel 4 was launched; Michael Jackson's *Thriller* album was released – it would go on to sell over

100 million copies and become the best-selling album in the world; David Puttnam's feature film *Chariots of Fire* won an Oscar for Best Picture; the Sinclair C5, a one-person battery-powered pedal bike, was launched, with the ambition of bringing electric vehicles to the masses for personal transport; *Back to the Future,* starring Michael J. Fox, became the highest grossing film ever in 1985; the Live Aid concerts raised £50 million in response to the Ethiopian famine; the M25 'London Orbital' motorway was opened; seatbelts became obligatory in the UK; Maradona's '*Hand of God*' goal (when his goal was allowed, despite the use of his hand) knocked England out of the FIFA World Cup in Mexico in 1986; *The Simpsons* was launched as a series of short animations in the *Tracy Ullman Show* in America; the Dalai Lama won the Nobel Peace Prize in recognition of his non-violent campaign to end the Chinese domination of Tibet; the Berlin Wall came down; and Nelson Mandela was released from prison after 27 years on Robben Island. Mandela had been sentenced to life imprisonment in 1962 by South Africa's ruling National Party's apartheid government for 'conspiring to overthrow the state'. Incredibly, despite his long years in prison, forced to break stones most days, he bore no ill feeling towards his captors. His kindness and gentleness inspired admiration worldwide; he was seen as the 'Man of the Century' and his release was celebrated around the world. The hope he inspired made it possible to believe this was the beginning of the end of racial segregation in South Africa.

Perhaps the most exciting development for the UK in this decade was the agreement signed between the UK and France in 1986 to go forward with their proposals to build the Channel Tunnel, which was opened to much fanfare in 1994, connecting Folkestone, England, with Coquelles, France. One of the many positive outcomes of this connection was the renovation of the former Midland Hotel (now the St Pancras Renaissance Hotel) in King's Cross. This splendid Victorian pile was built in 1873 by George Gilbert Scott, one of the outstanding architects of his day, but was now facing demolition. Thanks to the campaigning work of Sir John Betjeman and others in the 1960s it was spared. The onset of the Channel Tunnel led to it being finally restored to its former glory.

A beaming Queen Elizabeth opened the spectacular Eurostar rail terminal (which had previously been located at Waterloo) at King's Cross St Pancras in 2007, with inspiring, and optimistic words:

> *The remarkable re-birth of this great and gleaming station means people across the whole of Britain, not just the South-East, are suddenly quite a bit closer to Europe.*

> *And as we look forward to the London Olympics in 2012, it is good to know that a journey from here to the new High Speed 1 station at Stratford will take spectators a mere seven minutes.*

> *It gives me great pleasure to officially launch High Speed 1, Britain's first high speed railway and to re-open this magnificent station, St Pancras International.*

The journey time to Paris was just two hours and fifteen minutes.

The Queen also addressed a joint session of Congress in the United States – a first for a British Monarch – on 16 May 1991. She received three standing ovations and her 15-minute speech was wildly applauded. She finished:

> *All our history in this and earlier centuries underlines the basic point that the best progress is made when Europeans and Americans act in concert. We must not allow ourselves to be enticed into a form of continental insularity.*

# 1982

*The Queen's Christmas Broadcast in 1982 marked the fiftieth anniversary of the first Christmas message, and was filmed in the Library of Windsor Castle for the first time. The theme was 'the sea', in a year in which British troops went to war to defend the Falkland Islands in the South Atlantic.*

It is fifty years since the BBC External Service was started and my grandfather King George V made the first Christmas Broadcast from Sandringham. Today I am speaking to you from the Library at Windsor Castle, in a room that was once occupied by Queen Elizabeth I. This is my home, where for many years now my family and I have celebrated Christmas.

Within a few feet of where I am standing is the cliff, with its wonderful commanding view over the Thames, which led William the Conqueror to build a castle on this ideal defensive position – a castle that has to this day been the home of Kings and Queens.

In October I was in Brisbane for the Commonwealth Games and then went by sea in Britannia to visit a number of those beautiful Commonwealth island countries in the Pacific. At first sight, there does not appear to be much connection between a Norman castle, this Elizabethan gallery, the Commonwealth Games and the Pacific Islands. But in fact they are all linked by the sea.

William became the Conqueror after invading England by sea. It was the voyages of discovery by the great seamen of Queen Elizabeth's day which laid the foundations of modern trade; and to this day 90 per cent of it still goes by sea. Discovery and trade in their turn laid the foundations of the present-day Commonwealth. It was the development of ocean-going passenger vessels that allowed the peoples of the world to move about and to get to know each other. Such names as Drake, Anson, Frobisher, Cook, Vancouver and Phillip are familiar to people in widely different parts of the Commonwealth – while in Britain we owe our independence to the

*Opposite above:* Well-wishers waving British flags as they bid farewell to troops sailing on QE2 as it departs for the Falkland Islands. *Opposite below:* A happy and much relieved Queen on board the HMS Invincible, welcoming Prince Andrew back safely from the Falklands War. With them are Prince Philip and Princess Anne.

seamen who fought the Armada nearly 400 years ago and to Nelson and his band of brothers who destroyed Napoleon's dreams of invasion. Nor could the great battles for peace and freedom in the first half of the twentieth century have been won without control of the seas. Earlier this year in the South Atlantic the Royal Navy and the Merchant Navy enabled our sailors, soldiers and airmen to go to the rescue of the Falkland Islanders 8,000 miles across the ocean; and to reveal the professional skills and courage that could be called on in defence of basic freedoms.

Throughout history, seamen all over the world have shared a common experience and there is a special sense of brotherhood between merchant and naval seamen, fishermen, lifeboatmen and, more recently, yachtsmen. The navigators from the Pacific Islands, the fishermen of the Indian Ocean and China seas, and the men who man the oil rig supply ships in the North Atlantic have all learnt to come to terms with the varying moods of the seas and oceans.

*In a world more concerned with argument, the Games stand out as a demonstration of the better side of human nature.*

In much the same way, the members of the Commonwealth, which evolved from Britain's seafaring history, have acquired an affinity through sharing a common philosophy of individual freedom, democratic government and the rule of law.

It may not sound very substantial but when measured against the number and variety of inter-Commonwealth organisations and the multitude of commercial, medical, legal and sporting connections, it becomes clear that this common philosophy has had a very powerful influence for unity. Nothing could have demonstrated this unity more vividly than the immensely reassuring support given to Britain by the Commonwealth during the Falkland Islands crisis.

But the Commonwealth reveals its strength in many different ways. Any of you who attended or watched the events at the Commonwealth Games at Brisbane cannot have failed to notice the unique atmosphere of friendly rivalry and the generous applause for all the competitors.

In a world more concerned with argument, disagreement and violence, the Games stand out as a demonstration of the better side of human nature and of the great value of the Commonwealth as an association of free and independent nations. The Games also illustrated the consequences of the movement of peoples within the Commonwealth. Colour is no longer an indication of national origin. Until this century most racial and religious groups remained concentrated in their homelands but today almost every country of the Commonwealth has become multi-racial and multi-religious.

This change has not been without its difficulties, but I believe that for those with a sense of tolerance the arrival and proximity of different races and religions have provided a much better chance for each to appreciate the value of the others.

Three generations of the Royal Family greet the Wales's first child, Prince William.

At this time of the year, Christians celebrate the birth of their Saviour, but no longer in an exclusive way. We hope that our greetings at Christmas to all people of religious conviction and goodwill will be received with the same understanding that we try to show in receiving the greetings of other religious groups at their special seasons. The poet John Donne said: 'No man is an island, entire of itself; every man is a piece of the continent, a part of the main.'

That is the message of the Commonwealth and it is also the Christian message. Christ attached supreme importance to the individual and he amazed the world in which he lived by making it clear that the unfortunate and the underprivileged had an equal place in the Kingdom of Heaven with the rich and powerful. But he also taught that man must do his best to live in harmony with man and to love his neighbours.

In the Commonwealth, we are all neighbours and it is with this thought in mind that I wish you all, wherever you may be, the blessings of a happy and peaceful Christmas.

# 3 MARCH 1983
# STATE VISIT TO SAN FRANCISCO

*The Queen and Prince Philip spent a week in the Bay Area, and on their second night attended a dinner at the de Young Museum in Golden Bridge Park. The Queen replied to a speech from President Reagan.*

Mr. President, thank you for the very kind things you have said tonight. It is only nine months since we had the great pleasure of having you and Mrs. Reagan stay with us at Windsor. Now, we have had the memorable experience of visiting you in your home State of California and of seeing your ranch at Santa Barbara. I knew before we came that we had exported many of our traditions to the United States. But I had not realized before that weather was one of them. But, Mr. President, if the climate has been cool, your welcome and that of the American people have been wonderfully warm...

The past few days have been a vivid and sometimes poignant reminder of the human drama and achievement which account for the greatness of America today. We have seen some magnificent technological achievements – the space shuttle, which has begun to turn the adventure of space exploration into the equally adventurous but more tangible reality of scheduled space travel; Silicon Valley, which has brought the world of yesterday's science fiction into today's home, office, and classroom – and into Buckingham Palace, too.

This image of the United States at the forefront of technical invention is one of which you are rightly proud, as we are proud of our continued inventiveness in an era of pressing competition. But the miracle of the space shuttle or of the silicon chip lies not in the wizardry of electronics, but in the genius and shared, dedicated determination of men and women. That is what speaks loudest in California.

I think of the families who struggled against impossible odds, leaving their dead in places whose names still bear witness to their desperation to make their way to the west coast. In today's prosperity, their fortitude is often overlooked. But it is their character and courage which have permeated each succeeding generation.

I have seen that courage at work for myself this week, as many Californian families have coped valiantly with the hardship brought by the storms and tornado which have hit this State so hard...

In 1939, my father was the first reigning British sovereign to visit America, and he and President Roosevelt talked long and earnestly about the coming crisis. At the end of their visit, Mrs. Roosevelt wrote that 'in time of danger,' as she put it, 'something deeper comes to the surface and the British and we stand firmly together with confidence in our common heritage and ideas.'

By far the most important idea which we share is our belief in freedom ... It is an idea whose power is such that some men will go to as great lengths to suppress it as others will to keep it alive, as our two countries have fought to keep it alive...

We have had a visit which has been spectacular and has fulfilled a longstanding ambition on my part to visit California on the west coast. What better time than when the President is a Californian? We have enjoyed ourselves and greatly appreciate the warmth of your hospitality. What will remain afterwards is more significant — the cementing of a relationship. From time to time, friendships must be publicly reaffirmed. My visit has given me the opportunity to reaffirm the ideals which we share and the affection that exists between our people — without which the formalities of alliance would be meaningless, but from the certainty of which our two countries continue to draw strength.

President Reagan is highly amused by The Queen's reference to the bad, British-style weather that greeted her in California, during a state dinner held at the de Young Museum in San Francisco.

# 1983

*As the electronic age took off, The Queen's Christmas Broadcast in 1983 discussed the new possibilities for co-operation within the Commonwealth created by modern technologies. The Queen mentioned a visit to Bangladesh and India that year, in which she met Indian Prime Minister Indira Gandhi.*

In the year I was born, radio communication was barely out of its infancy; there was no television; civil aviation had hardly started and space satellites were still in the realm of science fiction. When my grandfather visited India in 1911, it took three weeks by sea to get there.

Last month I flew back from Delhi to London in a matter of hours. It took King George V three months to make the round trip. In two-thirds of that time Prince Philip and I were able to visit Jamaica, Mexico, the United States and Canada in the winter, followed by Sweden in the summer, and ending up in the autumn with Kenya, Bangladesh and finally India for the Commonwealth Heads of Government Meeting in New Delhi.

Travel and communication have entered a completely new dimension. In Los Angeles I went to see the space shuttle, which is playing such an important part in providing more and better international telecommunications. One of the tasks of that space shuttle was to launch an Indian telecommunications and weather satellite and last month I was able to see how this operated during our visit to an Earth Station in New Delhi.

All this astonishing and very rapid development has changed the lives of almost everyone. Leaders and specialists can meet and discuss political and technical problems; news travels faster and there is more of it; new opportunities for world trade and commerce have been opened up by this communication revolution; perhaps more important, modern technology has touched most aspects of life throughout the world.

We saw this in dramatic form in India. Twenty-two years ago I had seen something of the problems facing this vast country, but since then the population has grown from 440 million to over 700 million. Yet India has managed to become one of the ten or so leading industrial nations in the world and has become self-sufficient in food.

But in spite of all the progress that has been made the greatest problem in the world today remains the gap between rich and poor countries and we shall not begin to close this gap until we hear less about nationalism and more about interdependence. One of the main aims of the Commonwealth is to make an effective contribution towards redressing the economic balance between nations.

What we want to see is still more modern technology being used by poorer countries to provide employment and to produce primary products and components, which will be bought in turn by the richer countries at competitive prices.

I have therefore been heartened by the real progress that is being made through the Commonwealth Technical Cooperation Fund and various exchange schemes. Britain and other richer Commonwealth countries run aid schemes and these are very important, but the key word for the Commonwealth is cooperation.

During a royal tour of the US, The Queen visited Rockwell International Corporation in Los Angeles. Here she examines the Apollo 14 command module spacecraft. Apollo 14 was the third craft to land on the moon.

*We in the Commonwealth are fortunate enough to belong to a world wide comradeship. Let us make the most of it; let us all resolve to communicate as friends in tolerance and understanding.*

There is a flow of experts in all directions, with Canadians helping in the Caribbean, Indians in Africa, New Zealanders in India, Australians in Papua New Guinea, British in Kenya. The list is endless. The web of contacts provided by the Commonwealth is an intricate pattern based on self help and cooperation.

Yet in spite of these advances the age-old problems of human communication are still with us. We have the means of sending and receiving messages, we can travel to meetings in distant parts of the world, we can exchange experts; but we still have difficulty in finding the right messages to send, we can still ignore the messages we don't like to hear and we can still talk in riddles and listen without trying to comprehend.

Perhaps even more serious is the risk that this mastery of technology may blind us to the more fundamental needs of people. Electronics cannot create comradeship; computers cannot generate compassion; satellites cannot transmit tolerance. And no amount of technology could have engineered the spirit of the Commonwealth that was so evident in Delhi or the frank, friendly and understanding communication that such a spirit makes possible.

I hope that Christmas will remind us all that it is not how we communicate but what we communicate with each other that really matters. We in the Commonwealth are fortunate enough to belong to a world-wide comradeship. Let us make the most of it; let us all resolve to communicate as friends in tolerance and understanding. Only then can we make the message of the angels come true: 'Peace on earth, goodwill towards men'.

I always look forward to being able to talk to everyone at Christmas time and at the end of another year I again send you all my warmest greetings.

The Queen meets Mother Teresa at the Presidential Palace in
Delhi in November 1983, where she presented the
world-renown nun with the Order of Merit for her
humanitarian work.

# 1984

*The Queen welcomed her fourth grandchild, Prince Harry, and her Christmas Broadcast that year featured film of his christening. The theme of The Queen's message for that year was the lessons that adults could learn from children.*

Last June, we celebrated the fortieth anniversary of D-Day. That occasion in Normandy was a memorable one for all of us who were able to be there. It was partly a day of sadness, as we paid our respects to those who died for us, but it was also a day full of comradeship and hope.

For me, perhaps the most lasting impression was one of thankfulness that the forty intervening years have been ones of comparative peace.

The families of those who died in battle, and the veterans who fought beside them in their youth, can take comfort from the fact that the great nations of the world have contrived, sometimes precariously maybe, to live together without major conflict. The grim lessons of two World Wars have not gone completely unheeded.

I feel that in the world today there is too much concentration on the gloomy side of life, so that we tend to underestimate our blessings. But I think we can at least feel thankful that, in spite of everything, our children and grandchildren are growing up in a more or less peaceful world.

The happy arrival of our fourth grandchild gave great cause for family celebrations. But for parents and grandparents, a birth is also a time for reflection on what the future holds for the baby and how they can best ensure its safety and happiness.

To do that, I believe we must be prepared to learn as much from them as they do from us. We could use some of that sturdy confidence and devastating honesty with which children rescue us from self-doubts and self-delusions. We could borrow that unstinting trust of the child in its parents for our dealings with each other.

Above all, we must retain the child's readiness to forgive, with which we are all born and which it is all too easy to lose as we grow older. Without it, divisions between families, communities and nations remain unbridgeable. We owe it to our children and grandchildren to live up to the standards of behaviour and tolerance which we are so eager to teach them.

One of the more encouraging developments since the war has been the birth of the Commonwealth. Like a child, it has grown, matured and strengthened, until today the vision of its future is one of increasing understanding and co-operation between its members. Notwithstanding the strains and stresses of nationalism, different cultures and religions and its growing membership, the Commonwealth family has still managed to hold together and to make a real contribution to the prevention of violence and discord.

And it is not only in the Commonwealth that progress has been made towards a better understanding between nations. The enemies of 1944, against whom so many of our countrymen fought and died on those beaches in Normandy, are now our steadfast friends and allies.

But friendship, whether we are talking of continents or next door neighbours, should not need strife as its forerunner. It is particularly at Christmas, which marks the birth of the Prince of Peace, that we should work to heal old wounds and to abandon prejudice and suspicion. What better way of making a start than by remembering what Christ said – 'Except ye become as little children, ye shall not enter into the Kingdom of Heaven.' God bless you and a very happy Christmas to you all.

The Queen with world leaders on Omaha Beach, Normandy, gathered to commemorate the fortieth anniversary of D-Day landings: (from left) Canadian Prime Minister Pierre Trudeau; Queen Beatrix of the Netherlands; King Olav V of Norway; King Baudouin I of Belgium; French President Francois Mitterrand; The Queen; Jean, Grand Duke of Luxembourg and American President Ronald Reagan.

# 1985

*This year 1985 saw a devastating earthquake killing 10,000 in Mexico, a volcano killing 23,000 in Columbia, famine in Africa, and a plane crash off the coast of Ireland. The Queen's Christmas Broadcast emphasised on the good news stories of the year, praising remarkable public achievements.*

Looking at the morning newspapers, listening to the radio and watching television, it is only too easy to conclude that nothing is going right in the world.

All this year we seem to have had nothing but bad news with a constant stream of reports of plane crashes, earthquakes, volcanic eruptions and famine – and as if natural disasters were not enough, we hear of riots, wars, acts of terrorism and generally of man's inhumanity to man. It used to be said that 'no news is good news' but today you might well think that 'good news is no news'.

Yet there is a lot of good news and some wonderful things are going on in spite of the frightening headlines. Just think of the quiet courage and dedication of the peace-keepers and the rescue workers and all those who work so hard to restore shattered lives and disrupted communities.

I am in the fortunate position of being able to meet many of these people, for every year some two thousand come to Investitures at Buckingham Palace to be honoured for acts of bravery or to be recognised for service to their fellow citizens.

They come from all walks of life and they don't blow their own trumpets; so unless, like me, you are able to read the citations describing what they have done, you could not begin to guess at some of the remarkable stories that lie behind their visits to the Palace.

Among them there may be a really outstanding doctor who has worked for many years in a deprived area. Or a voluntary worker who has given nearly forty years of his life to campaigning for the disabled. Or a nurse, whose care for patients over thirty years

*Opposite above:* Members of the Royal Family watch the Trooping of the Colour during celebrations for The Queen's official birthday, 15 June. From left, The Queen Mother, The Duchess and Duke of Kent, Lord Frederick Windsor, Prince Philip, The Queen, Princess Anne, Prince Charles holding Prince Harry, Diana, Princess of Wales, and at the front Prince William, with some of his royal cousins. *Opposite below:* The Queen and Prince Philip with Sir Lynden Pindling, Prime Minister of the Bahamas, during The Commonwealth Heads of Government meeting in Nassau.

is a splendid example of the work done by members of a dedicated profession. Or another volunteer, who has devoted a large part of her life to others in the service of the WRVS.

Then there are those who have shown quite remarkable courage and devotion to duty. Only a few days ago I was talking to two firemen who had been called to deal with a blazing ship. They knew there were casualties below decks and despite the fact that both men were injured themselves, they risked the flames and smoke and further explosions and went below several times to bring the casualties to safety.

These are not exceptional cases. Every Investiture brings stories of bravery and self-sacrifice, like the members of bomb-disposal teams whose cool courage saves so many lives.

Naturally I see more such people in Britain, but as I often hold Investitures in other Commonwealth countries, I know that there are people making the same sort of good news all over the world.

But while bravery and service to the community are recognised by honours and awards, there are many ways in which people can make good news. Success in industry and commerce, for instance, creates the wealth that provides so many of the things that make life happier and more comfortable.

*I believe it is a time to look at the good things in life and to remember that there are a great many people trying to make the world a better place, even though their efforts may go unrecognised.*

It is not just the big companies with household names; quite small companies with only a few members can make a very significant contribution to the prosperity of their communities. The people in Britain who have helped their companies to success also come to the Palace as winners of The Queen's Awards for Export and Technology.

For example, last year there was a firm with only five employees, who make darts and export them to no less than forty countries! They were so enterprising that they introduced the game of darts into places where it had never been played.

Then there were the consulting engineers who won their award for technological achievement for their ingenious work on the Thames Flood Barrier. A small Scottish firm with eighteen employees make a product so good that they have sold their heating systems even in the United States and West Germany. Another firm has scored a rare double with their magnets for medical scanners, winning both the Awards – for Export and for Technology.

There are masses more, and it is encouraging to know that again next year there will be a new group coming to receive their awards, whose achievements will be just as ingenious and just as exciting. There are similar examples throughout the Commonwealth. These success stories are often pushed into the background but they are the guarantee of our future.

Christmas is a time of good news. I believe it is a time to look at the good things in life and to remember that there are a great many people trying to make the world a better place, even though their efforts may go unrecognised.

There is a lesson in this for us all and we should never forget our obligation to make our own individual contributions, however small, towards the sum of human goodness. The story of the Good Samaritan reminds us of our duty to our neighbour. We should try to follow Christ's clear instruction at the end of that story: 'Go and do thou likewise'. I wish you all a very happy Christmas and I hope that we shall all try to make some good news in the coming year.

# 1986

*This year saw the wedding of Prince Andrew to Sarah Ferguson in July at Westminster Abbey, who then assumed the titles Duke and Duchess of York. The Queen's Christmas Broadcast focussed on the spiritual side of the festival, reminding us that Christmas is above all a festival for children.*

Every year a Christmas party is held for the children of the people living in the Mews of Buckingham Palace. Everyone seems to enjoy it. Father Christmas arrives and there is the usual build up of excitement and expectation among the children to see what he has brought with him in his sack.

Even the horses in their stables are serenaded by the carol singers and seem to be aware that something quite special is happening — as they were on that happy day back in July when my son and daughter-in-law were married, and they drew the carriages through the cheerful crowds thronging the London streets.

For the children at our Christmas party, the meeting with Father Christmas, and a ride in his sleigh, are perhaps the most exciting part of the evening.

But I hope that a visit to the stables also helps to bring the traditional story alive for them. I hope it also helps them to realise how fortunate they are to have comfortable homes and warm beds to go to, unlike the Holy Family, who had to share with the animals because there was no room at the Inn.

Christmas is a festival for all Christians, but it is particularly a festival for children. As we all know, it commemorates the birth of a child, who was born to ordinary people, and who grew up very simply in his own small home town and was trained to be a carpenter.

His life thus began in humble surroundings, in fact in a stable, but he was to have a profound influence on the course of history, and on the lives of generations of his followers. You don't have to be rich or powerful in order to change things for the better and each of us in our own way can make a contribution.

The infant Jesus was fortunate in one very important respect. His parents were loving and considerate. They did their utmost to protect him from harm. They left their own home and became refugees, to save him from King Herod, and they brought him up according to the traditions of their faith.

On this birthday festival, which we try to make an occasion of happiness, we must not forget that there are some children who are victims of ill treatment and neglect. It is no easy task to care for and bring up children, whatever your circumstances– whether you are famous or quite unknown. But we could all help by letting the spirit of Christmas fill our homes with love and care and by heeding Our Lord's injunction to treat others as you would like them to treat you.

When, as the Bible says, Christ grew in wisdom and understanding, he began his task of explaining and teaching just what it is that God wants from us. The two lessons that he had for us, which he underlined in everything he said and did, are the messages of God's love and how essential it is that we, too, should love other people. There are many serious and threatening problems in this country and in the world but they will never be solved until there is peace in our homes and love in our hearts. The message which God sent us by Christ's life and example is a very simple one, even though it seems so difficult to put into practice.

To all of you, of every faith and race, I send you my best wishes for a time of peace and tranquillity with your families at this festival of Christmas. A very Happy Christmas to you all.

During a state visit to Shaanxi Province, China, The Queen inspects some of the 8,000 members of the Terracotta Army; astonishing, uniquely-featured statues of men and horses created in around 246 BC to guard the tomb of Emperor Qin Shi Huang.

# 1987

*In November of this year an IRA bomb exploded at a Remembrance Sunday service in Eniskillen, Northern Ireland, killing 12 people and injuring many more. One of the dead was Marie Wilson, whose father Gordon's astonishing words of forgiveness for the bombers touched hearts around the world, including The Queen's.*

Sooner or later we all become aware of the passing of the years, but every now and then we get a sharp reminder that time is moving on rather quicker than we expected. This happened to me last month when we celebrated our fortieth wedding anniversary. I was very touched that so many of you were kind enough to send messages of good wishes. There is no point in regretting the passage of time. Growing older is one of the facts of life, and it has its own compensations. Experience should help us to take a more balanced view of events and to be more understanding about the foibles of human nature.

*This year I hope we will continue to remember the many innocent victims of violence and intolerance and the sufferings of their families ... not just at Christmas, but all the year round.*

Like everyone else, I learn about what is going on in the world from the media, but I am fortunate to have another source of information. Every day hundreds of letters come to my desk, and I make a point of reading as many of them as I possibly can.

The vast majority are a pleasure to read. There are also sad ones from people who want help, there are interesting ones from people who want to tell me what they think about current issues, or who have suggestions to make about changing the way things are done. Others are full of frank advice for me and my family and some of them do not hesitate to be critical.

I value all these letters for keeping me in touch with your views and opinions, but there are a few letters which reflect the darker side of human nature. It is only too easy for passionate loyalty to one's own country, race or religion, or even to one's favourite football club, to be corroded into intolerance, bigotry and ultimately into violence. We have witnessed some frightening examples of this in recent years. All too often intolerance creates the resentment and anger which fill the headlines and divide communities and nations and even families.

From time to time we also see some inspiring examples of tolerance. Mr Gordon Wilson, whose daughter Marie lost her life in the horrifying explosion at Enniskillen on Remembrance Sunday, impressed the whole world by the depth of his forgiveness. His strength, and that of his wife, and the courage of their daughter, came from their Christian conviction. All of us will echo their prayer that out of the personal tragedies of Enniskillen may come a reconciliation between the communities.

The Queen with grandsons Harry and William, at guards Polo Club, Windsor, quite possibly watching their father Prince Charles compete.

There are striking illustrations of the way in which the many different religions can come together in peaceful harmony. Each year I try to attend the Commonwealth Day interfaith observance at Westminster Abbey. At that service all are united in their willingness to pray for the common good.

This is a symbol of mutual tolerance and I find it most encouraging. Of course it is right that people should hold their beliefs and their faiths strongly and sincerely, but perhaps we should also have the humility to accept that, while we each have a right to our own convictions, others have a right to theirs too.

I am afraid that the Christmas message of goodwill has usually evaporated by the time Boxing Day is over. This year I hope we will continue to remember the many innocent victims of violence and intolerance and the suffering of their families. Christians are taught to love their neighbours, not just at Christmas, but all the year round. I hope we will all help each other to have a happy Christmas and, when the New Year comes, resolve to work for tolerance and understanding between all people. Happy Christmas to you all.

# 1988

*In her Christmas Broadcast The Queen remarked on several historic anniversary celebrations that she attended. Then three major disasters occurred in December, after the Broadcast had been recorded, so The Queen added a further message to acknowledge these terrible events.*

In the year just past, Prince Philip and I have joined in the celebration of some notable anniversaries. The events which they marked were hundreds of years apart, but each was important enough to get much attention in 1988.

The earliest event which we remembered was the encounter with the Spanish Armada in 1588. The 400th anniversary fell in the same year in which we were able to mark the happy relations between Britain and Spain which now exist, by our state visit to Madrid. Four hundred years after 'the winds blew' and the Spanish ships were scattered, the events were remembered, without animosity, in both countries.

These prints from the Royal Library at Windsor illustrate the battles and some of the great fleet which gathered. This year, the present King of Spain showed me the rooms in the Escorial, where his predecessor, Philip the Second, planned the campaign. Had the fortunes of war gone against us, how very differently events in Britain and Europe would have unfolded.

Earlier in the year, we marked another event of the first importance in our history – the 300th anniversary of what is popularly known as the Glorious Revolution.

The invitation to King William and Queen Mary to accept the thrones of England and Scotland finally laid to rest the 'enterprise of England' which Philip of Spain set in hand. It thus gave the particular direction to our history which was to lead to the development of parliamentary democracy and the tradition of political and religious toleration which Britain enjoys today.

It was a great pleasure for us to celebrate that event in the company of the Crown Prince of the Netherlands. Together we visited Torbay – which was where King William landed in 1688. It was shrouded with fog when we were there, but we did manage to see through the mist some of the hundreds of British and Dutch yachts that had assembled there.

Three hundred years may seem a long time ago, but there are still some objects here in Buckingham Palace which bring to life William and Mary as people – and one

The Queen opens World Expo 88 in Brisbane in April, during her
tour of Australia. She stands with Prime Minister Hawke and his
first wife, Hazel.

which I particularly treasure is this little patch box that belonged to Queen Mary and which caries her monogram entwined with William's on the lid.

The 1988 anniversary season opened in Australia – with a grand party on Australia Day to mark the country's 200th birthday. It was a party which went on for most of the year, but Prince Philip and I joined in the festivities in April and May. Like so many visitors in bicentennial year, we brought home some souvenirs of our visit. In our case it was some delightful early prints of Sydney, which served to remind us of the extraordinary developments which have taken place in Australia in the short space of two hundred years.

Contrast this scene of Sydney Harbour with the pictures we all saw of the crowded waters around the Opera House and the famous bridge in January this year.

Centenaries may seem rather arbitrary occasions, but they nonetheless prompt us to look back into the past. When we do so, we can draw hope from seeing how ancient enmities have vanished; and how new nations have grown and established themselves in vigour and wisdom. Equally, they make us reflect on injustices and tragedies and inspire us to do our best to learn from these as well. To do that, we surely should draw inspiration from one other anniversary – the one we celebrate every year at this time, the birth of Christ.

In May 1988, The Queen unveiled a statue of herself at the opening of the new Australian Parliament House in Canberra.

There are many grand and splendid pictures in the Royal Collection that illustrate this event, but one which gives me particular pleasure is this precious, almost jewel-like book. It is a 'Book of Hours', full of prayers and devotional readings. It's in Latin, but it contains the most exquisite illuminations and it is these that speak to us most movingly.

The anonymous person who drew the pictures nearly five hundred years ago has included all the familiar elements of the Christmas story which we hear with such pleasure every year. Here are the angels, bringing the glad tidings to the shepherds, who listen attentively. Down here, where baby Jesus lies in the stall, you can see Mary and Joseph, watching over him, quite unmoved, it seems, by the man playing the bagpipes overhead. The star over the stable has lit the way for all of us ever since, and there should be no one who feels shut out from that welcoming and guiding light. The legends of Christmas about the ox and the ass suggest that even the animals are not outside that loving care.

Recently, many of you will have set up and decorated a Christmas tree in your homes. Often these are put by a window and the bright and shining tree is there for every passer-by to see and share. I like to think that if someone who feels lonely and unloved should see such a tree, that person might feel: 'It was meant for me'.

May the Christmas story encourage you, for it is a message of hope every year, not for a few, but for all.

So in sending you my Christmas greeting, I pray that God may bless you – every one.

As you probably all know, my Christmas Broadcast has to be recorded well before Christmas Day so that it can be made available to radio and television stations throughout the Commonwealth.

Since I made that recording this year, we have all been shocked and distressed by a series of major disasters: here in Britain, the worst air crash in our history at Lockerbie and a serious train accident at Clapham; and in Armenia, a terrible earthquake.
All three came with great suddenness and destroyed the lives of many people who were looking forward to celebrating Christmas with their families and friends. So there are many homes today where the joy of Christmas has been darkened by a cloud of sadness and grief.

Our hearts and prayers go out to those who have been injured or bereaved, and it is my hope that the eternal message of Christmas will bring some comfort in the hour of sadness.

# 1989

*This year The Queen chose to focus on climate change and fears for the future of the planet, specifically how this will impact on our children, and the role they can play to save it. The Broadcast was recorded in the Royal Albert Hall, London, at a Save The Children charity event.*

I usually make my Christmas Broadcast to the Commonwealth from Windsor or Buckingham Palace. This year I thought I would use the presence of two thousand children at this occasion organised by Save the Children Fund in the Albert Hall, here in the heart of London, to send this special message to the children of the Commonwealth. Those of you present are the immediate audience for my broadcast, but I am also speaking by radio and television to people throughout the world.

All parents would like their children to grow up in peace and tranquillity, but for most of this century the people of this world have had to live through bewildering changes and upheavals. Some of the changes have been for the better, but others might even threaten the world we live in. There are some children who are much less fortunate than others, for they come from countries where nature makes life very hard, with floods and droughts and other disasters destroying crops, making it very difficult to find enough for everyone to eat. Quite a lot of you have written to me during the last year or so, saying how worried you are about the future of our planet.

Many of you will have heard of the greenhouse effect, and perhaps you've heard too about even more urgent problems caused by the pollution of our rivers and seas and the cutting down of the great forests. These problems don't affect just the countries where they are happening and they make neighbourly co-operation throughout the world a pressing necessity. With all your lives before you, I am sure that you take an optimistic view of the future. But it is already too late to prevent all forms of damage to the natural world. Some species of wild plants and animals are, sadly, bound to become extinct. But the great thing to remember is that it is not too late to reduce the damage if we change attitudes and behaviour.

You've all seen pictures of the earth taken from space. Unlike all the other planets in the solar system, earth shimmers green and blue in the sunlight and looks a very pleasant place to live. These pictures should remind us that the future of all life on earth depends on how we behave towards one another, and how we treat the plants and the animals that share our world with us.

Men and women have shown themselves to be very clever at inventing things, right back to the time when they found out how much easier it was to move things about on wheels, up to the present time when rockets and computers make it possible for people to travel away from our world into the mystery of space.

But these technical skills are not enough by themselves. They can only come to the rescue of the planet if we also learn to live by the golden rule that Jesus Christ taught us – 'love thy neighbour as thyself'.

Many of you will have heard the story of the Good Samaritan, and of how Christ answered the question (from a clever lawyer who was trying to catch him out) 'who is my neighbour?' Jesus told of the traveller who was mugged and left injured on the roadside where several important people saw him, and passed by without stopping to help. His neighbour was the man who did stop, cared for him, and made sure he was being well looked after before he resumed his own journey. It's not very difficult to apply that story to our own times and to work out that our neighbours are those of our friends, or complete strangers, who need a helping hand. Do you think they might also be some of the living species threatened by spoiled rivers, or some of the children in places like Ethiopia and Sudan who don't have enough to eat?

*You children have something to give us which is priceless. You can still look at the world with a sense of wonder and remind us grown-ups that life is wonderful and precious.*

The exciting news of the last few months has been the way in which people in both East and West Europe have begun to think about the future in a less unfriendly way — more as neighbours. It's still hard for us to be sure what is going to happen as a result of these great events, but it would be splendid to think that in the last years of the twentieth century Christ's message about loving our neighbours as ourselves might at last be heeded.

If it is, they'll be good years for you to grow up in. If we can reduce selfishness and jealousy, dishonesty and injustice, the nineties can become a time of peace and tranquillity for children and grown-ups, and a time for working together for the benefit of our planet as a whole.

You children have something to give us which is priceless. You can still look at the world with a sense of wonder and remind us grown-ups that life is wonderful and precious. Often a child's helplessness and vulnerability bring out the best in us. Part of that 'best in us' could be a particular tenderness towards this earth which we share as human beings, all of us, and, together, as the nations of the world, will leave to our children and our children's children. We must be kind to it for their sake. In the hope that we will be kind and loving to one another, not just on Christmas Day, but throughout the year, I wish you all a very Happy Christmas. God bless you.

# 1990

*This year The Queen contrasted the happiness of the celebrations for The Queen Mother's ninetieth birthday with other darker events around the globe, including the invasion of Kuwait and the threat of war in the Middle East.*

Over the years, I have dwelt on the happier side of life in my Christmas Broadcasts — we need reminding of it, particularly at Christmas time. This year, there have been, I hope, times of happiness and good cheer for most of us.

My family, for instance, has been celebrating my mother's ninetieth birthday, and we have shared with you the joy of some of those celebrations.

My youngest grandchild's christening, two days ago, has brought the family together once again. I hope that all of us lucky enough to be able to enjoy such gatherings this Christmas will take time to count our blessings. For it seems to me that there is one deep and overriding anxiety for us all on which we should reflect today. That is the threat of war in the Middle East.

The servicemen in the Gulf who are spending Christmas at their posts under this threat are much in our thoughts. And there are many others, at home and abroad, servicemen and civilians, who are away from their own firesides. Wherever they are, may they all, when their duty is done, soon be reunited with their families safe and sound.

At the same time we must remember those still held hostage. Some of them have spent years in captivity, and Christmas must, for them, be especially hard to bear. My heart goes out to them and to their families. We can, at least, rejoice at the safe return of many of their compatriots over the last weeks, and salute the courage which they have shown.

Wars, threats of wars and civil disturbance inevitably cause thousands of innocent people to become refugees and to have their lives ruined or disrupted. It is difficult for us, safe at home, to contemplate the scale of the suffering for homeless and hungry people caused by the ever-widening consequences of the crisis in the Gulf. The invasion of Kuwait was an example on an international scale of an evil which has beset us at different levels in recent years – attempts by ruthless people to impose their will on the peaceable majority.

Soldiers of the Fifth Airborne Brigade of the Parachute Regiment put on a good show for their Colonel-in-Chief on Salisbury Plain, Wiltshire, during her inspection in May.

The Queen Mother enjoys her ninetieth birthday in 1990 with members of her family at Clarence House in London. With The Queen are Prince Edward, The Princess and Prince of Wales and Princess Margaret.

In extreme form, as we know only too well, these attempts lead to disaster and death, and their tragic aftermath for families and communities. In the United Kingdom, we have suffered once again during the past year from the scourge of terrorism, its disregard for human life and its efforts to dress its crimes in political clothes. But all this is nothing new. The tributes we paid last summer to the heroes of Dunkirk and the Battle of Britain were tributes to their achievement in repelling a determined invader. That was fifty years ago.

Nowadays there are all too many causes that press their claims with a loud voice and a strong arm rather than with the language of reason. We must not allow ourselves to be too discouraged as we confront them. Let us remember that Christ did not promise the earth to the powerful. The resolve of those who endure and resist these activities should not be underestimated.

*Nowadays there are all too many causes that press their claims with a loud voice and a strong arm rather than with the language of reason. We must not allow ourselves to be too discouraged as we confront them.*

I never cease to admire the stoical courage of those in Northern Ireland, for example, who go about their business in defiance of the terrorist. The reaction of those who have lost loved ones at violent hands is often an inspiration to the rest of us.

Then again, I, like many others, was much heartened by the virtually unanimous opposition of the international community to the unprovoked invasion of Kuwait, and by the speed with which moves were made to try to relieve the plight of the innocent victims.

I want, therefore, to say thank you today to the men and women who, day in and day out, carry on their daily life in difficult and dangerous circumstances. By just getting on with the job, they are getting the better of those who want to harm our way of life.

Let us think of them this Christmas, wherever they are in the world, and pray that their resolution remains undiminished. It is they and their kind who, by resisting the bully and the tyrant, ensure that we live in the sort of world in which we can celebrate this season safely with our families.

I pray also that we may all be blessed with something of their spirit. Then we would find it easier to solve our disputes in peace and justice, wherever they occur, and that inheritance of the earth which Christ promised, not to the strong, but to the meek, would be that much closer. A Happy Christmas and God bless you all.

# 16 May 1991
# ADDRESS TO THE US CONGRESS

*At a few minutes to noon in Washington, The Queen spoke to a packed joint session of Congress. It was the first such address by a British monarch. She received rapturous applause at several points, and three standing ovations!*

I do hope you can see me today from where you are. Mr.Speaker, Mr.President, Distinguished Members of Congress, I know what a rare privilege it is to address a joint meeting of your two Houses. Thank you for inviting me.

The concept, so simply described by Abraham Lincoln as 'government by the people, of the people, for the people', is fundamental to our two nations. Your Congress and our Parliament are the twin pillars of our civilizations and the chief among the many treasures that we have inherited from our predecessors…

Some people believe that power grows from the barrel of a gun. So it can. But history shows that it never grows well nor for very long. Force, in the end, is sterile. We have gone a better way. Our societies rest on mutual agreement, on contract and on consensus. A significant part of your social contract is written down in your Constitution. Ours rests on custom and will. The spirit behind both, however, is precisely the same. It is the spirit of democracy.

These ideals are clear enough, but they must never be taken for granted. They have to be protected and nurtured through every change and fluctuation. I want to take this opportunity to express the gratitude of the British people to the people of the United States of America for their steadfast loyalty to our common enterprise throughout this turbulent century.

The future is, as ever, obscure. The only certainty is that it will present the world with new and daunting problems, but … I have every confidence that we can resolve them. Recent events in the Gulf have proved that it is possible to do just that. Both our countries saw the invasion of Kuwait in just the same terms; an outrage to be reversed, both for the people of Kuwait and for the sake of the principle that naked aggression should not prevail. Our views were identical and so were our responses. That response was not without risk, but we have both learned from history that we must not allow aggression to succeed.

I salute the outstanding leadership of your President, and the courage and prowess of the armed forces of the United States. I know that the servicemen and women of Britain, and of all the members of the coalition, were proud to act in a just cause alongside their American comrades. Unfortunately, experience shows that great enterprises seldom end with a tidy and satisfactory flourish…

For all that uncertainty, it would be a mistake to make the picture look too gloomy. The swift and dramatic changes in Eastern Europe in the last decade have opened up great opportunities for the people of those countries. They are finding their own paths to freedom. But the paths would have been blocked if the Atlantic Alliance had not stood together — if your country and mine had not stood together. Let us never forget that lesson. …

All our history in this and earlier centuries underlines the basic point that the best progress is made when Europeans and Americans act in concert. We must not allow ourselves to be enticed into a form of continental insularity…

Our two countries have a special advantage in seeking to guide the process of change because of the rich ethnic and cultural diversity of both our societies. Stability in our own countries depends on tolerance and understanding between different communities. Perhaps we can, together, build on our experience to spread the message we have learned at home to those regions where it has yet to be absorbed.

Whether we will be able to realize our hopes will depend on the maintenance of an acceptable degree of international order. In this we see the United Nations as the essential instrument in the promotion of peace and cooperation. We look to its Charter as the guardian of civilized conduct between nations…

We want to build on that foundation and to do better. And, if the going gets rough, I hope you can still agree with your poet Emerson, who wrote in 1847, 'I feel, in regard to this aged England, with a kind of instinct, that she sees a little better on a cloudy day, and that, in storm of battle and calamity, she has a secret vigor and a pulse like a cannon.' You will find us worthy partners, and we are proud to have you as our friends. May God bless America.

# 1991

*In 1991 Boris Yeltsin won the first public elections to be held in Russia, ushering in a new era of East-West relations. The United States and the Soviet Union signed an historic agreement to reduce their stockpiles of nuclear warheads. The Queen's Christmas Broadcast reflected on these enormous changes.*

In 1952, when I first broadcast to you at Christmas, the world was a very different place to the one we live in today. Only seven years had passed since the end of the most destructive wars in the history of mankind. Even the end of the hostilities did not bring the true peace for which so many had fought and died. What became known as the 'Cold War' sustained an atmosphere of suspicion, anxiety and fear for many years.

Then, quite suddenly, everything began to change, and the changes have happened with bewildering speed. In 1989 the Berlin Wall came down. Since then the rest of the world has watched, fascinated, as oppressive regimes have crumbled under popular pressure. One by one, these liberated peoples have taken the first hesitant, and sometimes painful, steps towards open and democratic societies.

Naturally, we welcome this, and it may be that we can help them achieve their aims. But, in doing that, we need to remind ourselves of the essential elements which form the bedrock of our own free way of life – so highly valued and so easily taken for granted.

This can be an opportunity to reflect on our good fortune, and on whether we have anything to offer by way of example to those who have recently broken free of dictatorship. We, who claim to be of the free world, should examine what we really mean by freedom, and how we can help to ensure that, once in place, it is there to stay.

There are all sorts of elements to a free society, but I believe that among the most important is the willingness of ordinary men and women to play a part in the life of their community, rather than confining themselves to their own narrow interests.

Vice President Dan Quayle (left) and Speaker of the House of Representatives Thomas Foley applaud as The Queen addresses a joint meeting of the US Senate and the House of Representatives in Washington in May.

*There are all sorts of elements to a free society, but I believe that among the most important is the willingness of ordinary men and women to play a part in the life of their community, rather than confining themselves to their own narrow interests.*

The parts they play may not be major ones – indeed they can frequently turn out to be thankless tasks. The wonder is, though, that there are so many who are prepared to devote much of their lives, for no reward, to the service of their fellow men and women. Without their dedication, where would our churches and charities be, for instance? Without such people, many would be unable to enjoy the pleasure which the arts bring to our daily lives. Governments can encourage and support, but it is the volunteers who work away for nothing in administration or spend their weekends seeing fair play, who make sport and physical recreation so worthwhile.

I am constantly amazed by the generosity of donors and subscribers, great and small, who give so willingly and often towards the enjoyment of others. Without them these voluntary organisations simply would not exist.

The peoples of the former Soviet Union and Eastern Europe have broken the mould of autocracy. I hope that we will be able to help them as they learn that the democracy that has replaced it depends, not on political structures, but on the goodwill and the sense of responsibility of each and every citizen. It is not, of course, as simple as that. All the selfless voluntary work in the world can be wasted if it disregards the views and aspirations of others. There are any number of reasons to find fault with each other, with our Governments, and with other countries.

But let us not take ourselves too seriously. None of us has a monopoly of wisdom and we must always be ready to listen and respect other points of view. At the Commonwealth Heads of Government Meeting in Zimbabwe this autumn, we saw an example of mutual tolerance and respect for the views of others on an international scale. Leaders of the fifty nations came together to discuss the future.

They met in peace, they talked freely, they listened, they found much on which to agree, and they set a new direction for the Commonwealth. I am sure that each derived strength and reassurance in the process. That was just one event in a year of massive and historic change. This time last year we were thinking of the servicemen and women in the Gulf, and of the hostages in captivity. Our prayers for their safe homecoming have largely been answered.

This Christmas we can take heart in seeing how, in the former Soviet Union and Eastern Europe, where it has endured years of persecution and hardship, the Christian faith is once again thriving and able to spread its message of unselfishness, compassion and tolerance.

Next February will see the fortieth anniversary of my father's death and of my Accession. Over the years I have tried to follow my father's example and to serve you as best I can.

You have given me, in return, your loyalty and your understanding, and for that I give you my heartfelt thanks. I feel the same obligation to you that I felt in 1952. With your prayers, and your help, and with the love and support of my family, I shall try to serve you in the years to come. May God bless you and bring you a Happy Christmas.

The Royal Family attend a Christmas service in 1991 at Sandringham, Norfolk. From left, Diana, Princess of Wales, Princes William and Harry, Queen Elizabeth The Queen Mother, Sarah, Duchess of York, Prince Philip, and Princess Margaret.

# 1992 ~ 2001

## *Into*
## THE NEW
## MILLENNIUM

The Queen and Prince Philip on their way to the
State Opening of Parliament in 2000.

This decade has proved one of the most defining of The Queen's reign so far. Tim Berners-Lee, an English computer scientist shared with the world his pioneering work in what became known as the world wide web. In the spirit of the early pioneers of computing he released it on the internet for free between 1991 and 1993. It was the single most significant innovation of the century and single-handedly changed the way we work and play. Fast-forward to 2021, where there were 4.7 billion globally active users – 60 percent of the world's population – mostly (92 percent) accessing it via a mobile device.

In 1997 The Labour Party finally won a general election, having last been in power between 1974 and 1979. The party was led by Tony Blair, a boyish-looking, dynamic and charismatic leader. Labour won by 418 seats to 165 (Conservative); a landslide, and a rejuvenated Liberal Democrats party also fared well, winning 46 seats.

And then…

Diana, Princess of Wales, who had divorced Prince Charles just a year earlier, was killed in a car crash in Paris, in the early hours of 31 August 1997, aged 36.  Diana's death rocked the royal family and made us all ponder whether the concept and nature of the monarchy had passed its sell-by date.

For five days the royal family – The Queen and Prince Philip, Prince Charles with his sons William (15) and Harry (13) hunkered down in their Balmoral bunker, while thousands of ordinary people wept openly for Diana, who had captured their hearts. There were many poor decisions made by the royals during that time. By contrast. Prime Minister Blair, assisted by his close aide Alastair Campbell, caught the public mood, calling Diana, the *People's Princess*. The empty flagpole at Buckingham Palace without a flag at half-mast was seemingly the last straw for sections of the media, who felt the royal family lacked understanding of the nation's grief. For perhaps the first time, The Queen had put her family's needs ahead of the nation's.

Eventually The Queen returned to Buckingham Palace on Friday 5 September, a day earlier than expected, and seeing the huge crowds and the wall of flowers for the late Princess Diana, had her car stop just short of the gates. To onlookers' surprise,

The Queen and Prince Philip stepped out into the crowd, who were uncertain how to react. Then, the tense silence was broken by a small amount of clapping, which softened the mood. It was a turning point.

That evening The Queen addressed the nation

*First, I want to pay tribute to Diana myself. She was an exceptional and gifted human being. In good times and bad, she never lost her capacity to smile and laugh, nor to inspire others with her warmth and kindness. I admired and respected her – for her energy and commitment to others, and especially her devotion to her two boys…*

Away from the royal sphere, there was a compelling new crop of young artists who dominated the art world throughout the 1990s. Many were alumni of Goldsmiths College under the leadership of conceptual artist and painter Michael Craig-Martin. These emerging artists sheltered under the 'Young British Artists' label, though there was no set 'manifesto'. Among the best known are Damien Hirst and Tracey Emin. The group benefitted from their close association with advertising guru Charles Saatchi, who was the artists' biggest fan and collector. 'Controversy' became their watchword.

In 1994, the state-franchised National Lottery was launched. An initiative of Prime Minister John Major, it has proved an unqualified success. Later, to celebrate the upcoming millennium, special awards were given for new ideas across the nation. These included the renovation of a disused power station opposite St Paul's Cathedral in London to create Tate Modern; the Eden Project in Cornwall,; the extraordinary Falkirk Wheel, a rotating boat lift in central Scotland; the potentially world-saving Millenium Seed Bank in West Sussex; a new Millennium Stadium in Cardiff and the Millenium Dome (now the 02 Centre) in London.

This decade experienced several wars, but two in particular stood out. As Yugoslavia broke up in the middle of 1991, calamity set in across the region and lasted a decade. The Siege of Sarajevo (1992-1995) led to ethnic cleansing, war rape, genocide and huge losses of civilian properties Perhaps as many as 140,000 people were killed, 2.4 million refugees were created and a further 600,000 people were displaced. It was a stain on humanity.

There was worse to come, with large-scale genocide between the Hutu and Tutsi tribes in Rwanda taking place over four years, eventually ending in 1994. It was terrifying. Over half a million people were killed, representing two thirds of the Tutsi population in Rwanda. Maybe as many as 500,000 women were raped and many who survived were found to be HIV positive. There were two milllion refugees The United Nations was a bystander.

The world welcomed and celebrated the start of the third millennium on 1 January 2000 with some nations like the UK and Australia putting on spectacular firework displays. In the UK, the Millennium Dome was the centre of Britain's celebrations. Unfortunately, the ticketing on the 'One Amazing Night' meant thousands queuing for hours to gain entrance. Visibility was not good enough to risk Concorde flying over central London and the new Millennium Wheel, now known as the London Eye, though formally

opened that day was not fully operational until March 2000. Despite these setbacks, on the stroke of midnight as 1999 became the year 2000, the large, invited crowd sang *Auld Lang Syne* and the look between The Queen and Prime Minister Blair as they tried to link hands to sing was apparently one of happiness. Most of us were just relieved that the expected 'Y2K' Millennium Bug did not play havoc with the world's computers and computer networks.

There was another bug of sorts when the nation was assailed by an outbreak of foot-and-mouth disease amongst its livestock, lasting from February to October 2001. It caused the postponement of the General Election by a month and exposed the dubious practices of some elements of the farming industry. Four million diseased animals (mainly sheep but also over half a million cattle and pigs) were slaughtered, and a further two million healthy animals were destroyed because they could not be moved for fear of spreading the disease.

But these era-defining events and activities were wholly eclipsed by the sustained attack on America on what became known as 9/11 (11 September 2001), when al-Qaeeda operatives hijacked four commercial aeroplanes to use as lethal weapons. Two jets were crashed into the twin towers of World Trade Center in New York, which collapsed; another rammed into the west side of the Pentagon in Washington DC and the fourth, possibly heading for the White House or the US Capitol building (this is still unknown), crashed in a field near Shanksville, Pennsylvania, as passengers bravely tried to wrest control from the hijackers. In total, 2,977 people died and over 25,000 were injured. It is estimated that damage to the infrastructure topped $10 billion.

Revenge was in the air.

# 1992

*The Queen described her Ruby Jubilee as her 'annus horribilis'. The Duke and Duchess of York separated, Princess Anne and Captain Mark Phillips were divorced and the rifts between the Prince and Princess of Wales were exposed to merciless public gaze. Then in November, a fire devastad Windsor Castle.*

This year, I am speaking to you not from Buckingham Palace, but from Sandringham, where my family gathers every year for Christmas. My great-grandfather, King Edward VII, made Sandringham his country home in 1862, and it was from this house that my grandfather, King George V, and my father, used to speak over the radio – originally to the Empire and then to the Commonwealth – on Christmas Day all those years ago.

It was from here that I made my first Christmas Broadcast forty years ago, and this year I am very glad to be able to speak to you again from this family home. I first came here for Christmas as a grandchild. Nowadays, my grandchildren come here for the same family festival. To me, this continuity is a great source of comfort in a world of change, tension and violence. The peace and tranquillity of the Norfolk countryside make me realise how fortunate we are, and all the more conscious of the trials and sorrows that so many people are suffering both in this country and around the world. My heart goes out to those whose lives have been blighted by war, terrorism, famine, natural disaster or economic hardship.

Like many other families, we have lived through some difficult days this year. The prayers, understanding and sympathy given to us by so many of you, in good times and bad, have lent us great support and encouragement. It has touched me deeply that much of this has come from those of you who have troubles of your own.

As some of you may have heard me observe, it has, indeed, been a sombre year. But Christmas is surely the right moment to try to put it behind us and to find a moment to pray for those, wherever they are, who are doing their best in all sorts of ways to make things better in 1993. I am thinking especially of the servicemen and women, and the aid workers with them, trying to keep the peace in countries riven by strife, and to bring food to the weak and innocent victims. They do not have an easy task and they need all the moral and practical support that we can give them.

Curiously enough, it was a sad event which did as much as anything in 1992 to help me put my own worries into perspective. Just before he died, Leonard Cheshire came to see us with his fellow members of the Order of Merit. By then, he was suffering from a long drawn-out and terminal illness. He bore this with all the fortitude and cheerfulness to be expected of a holder of the Victoria Cross. However, what struck me more forcibly than his physical courage was the fact that he made no reference to his own illness, but only to his hopes and plans to make life better for others. He embodied the message in those well-known lines: 'Kindness in another's trouble, courage in one's own'.

One of his Cheshire Homes for people with disabilities is not far from this house. I have visited others all over the Commonwealth and I have seen at first hand the remarkable results of his, and his wife's, determination to put Christ's teaching to practical effect. Perhaps this shining example of what a human being can achieve in a lifetime of dedication can inspire in the rest of us a belief in our own capacity to help others.

Such talents and indomitable spirit are not given to all of us. But if we can sometimes lift our eyes from our own problems, and focus on those of others, it will be at least

In November, a devastating fire at Windsor Castle destroyed 155 rooms. The blaze began in Queen Victoria's Chapel, when a faulty spotlight ignited a curtain. Fortunately no one was hurt, but restoration work took five years.

The Queen arriving at an event in Earl's Court to celebrate the fortieth anniversary of her accession to the throne.

a step in the right direction, and Christmas is a good time to take it. I hope that his example will continue to inspire us all in the years ahead.

1993 will certainly bring new challenges, but let us resolve to meet it with fresh hope in our hearts. There is no magic formula that will transform sorrow into happiness, intolerance into compassion or war into peace, but inspiration can change human behaviour. Those, like Leonard Cheshire, who devote their lives to others, have that inspiration and they know, and we know, where to look for help in finding it. That help can be readily given if we only have the faith to ask. I and my family, as we approach a new year, will draw strength from this faith in our commitment to your service in the coming years.

I pray that each and every one of you has a happy Christmas and that we can all try to bring that happiness to others. God bless you all.

# 1993

*This year, The Queen chose again to speak from the library at Sandringham, taking
the fascinating collection of her family's books as a starting point for her Broadcast.
She also reflected on the world as a 'global village' in which we should all play a part,
praising those engaged in international charity work.*

Four generations of my family have enjoyed the quiet and solitude of this library
at Sandringham. It is still a haven of peace even if my grandchildren do their best
over Christmas to make it rather more lively!

Most of the books on the shelves date from my great-grandfather's time, and their
titles reflect the life and events of those days. Books are one of the ways in which
each generation can communicate its history, values and culture to the next. There
are books here about statesmen, explorers, warriors and saints; there are many about
war, especially the First World War which ended seventy-five years ago. Families and
loved ones of those who fought in it knew little of the horrors of the trenches, other
than from artists' drawings or photographs – often published days or weeks after the
event. Nowadays stories and pictures from all over the world can be gathered up and
appear in print within hours.

We have indeed become a global village. It is no longer possible to plead ignorance
about what is going on in far-off parts of the world. Switch on the television or radio,
and the graphic details of distant events are instantly available to us.

Not all the pictures bring gloomy news. This year has seen significant progress made
towards solving some of the world's most difficult problems – the Middle East,
for instance, the democratic future of South Africa and, most recently, Northern
Ireland. All too often, though, we find ourselves watching or listening to the sort of
news which, as a daily diet, can be almost overwhelming. It makes us yearn for some
good news.

If we can look on the bright side, so much the better, but that does not mean we
should shield ourselves from the truth, even if it is unwelcome. I believe that we
should be aware of events which, in the old days, might have passed us by. But that
means facing up to the question of what we can do to use that awareness for the
greater good. The simple answer is, of course, all too little. But there is another
answer. It is that the more we know, the more we feel responsible, and the more we
want to help.

Those involved in international charity work confirm that modern communications have helped to bring them public support and made them more effective. People are not shunning the added responsibility, but shouldering it. All of us owe a debt to those volunteers who are out there in the front line, putting our donations to use by looking after the wounded, the hungry and the oppressed. Much of their work never reaches the headlines or television screens, but their example should inspire us all the same.

*We can all read that message of hope in our own lives, in our actions and in our prayers. If we do, the reflection may light the way for others and help them to read the message too.*

We cannot all follow them the whole way, but we can do something to help within our own community – particularly at Christmas, when those without work, or the company of family or friends, feel especially left out. I am always moved by those words in St. John's Gospel, which we hear on Christmas Day: 'He was in the world, and the world was made by him, and the world knew him not'. We have only to listen to the news to know the truth of that. But the Gospel goes on: 'But as many as received him, to them gave he power to become the sons of God'.

For all the inhumanity around us, let us be grateful for those who have received him and who go about quietly doing their work and His will without thought of reward or recognition. They know that there is an eternal truth of much greater significance than our own triumphs and tragedies, and it is embodied by the Child in the Manger. That is their message of hope.

We can all try to reflect that message of hope in our own lives, in our actions and in our prayers. If we do, the reflection may light the way for others and help them to read the message too. We live in the global village, but villages are made up of families. We, the peoples of the fifty nations of the Commonwealth – more than a quarter of the world's population – have, as members of one of the largest families, a great responsibility. By working together, we can help the rest of the world become a more humane and happier place. I hope you all enjoy your Christmas. I pray, with you, for a happy and peaceful New Year.

The Queen with the Bishop of Bath and Wells as she attends a Maunday Service at Wells Cathedral. This service, which commemorates Christ washing the feet of his disciples at The Last Supper, takes place on Maundy Thursday before Easter. The Queen distributes special Maundy money to recipients who have been nominated for their services to their local church and community.

# 1994

*In her Broadcast this year The Queen spoke movingly of witnessing D-Day commemorations in France, and in Russia, where she and Prince Philip visited St Petersburg to join a service to honour the millions of Russians who died fighting Nazism in World War II.*

I shall never forget the events in Normandy last June, when the representatives of the wartime allies commemorated the fiftieth anniversary of the D-Day landings. We who were there, and millions of others through television and radio, paid fitting tribute to the courage of those who took part in that epic campaign.

As Prince Philip and I stood watching the British veterans march past on the beach at Arromanches, my own memories of 1944 were stirred – of how it was to wait anxiously for news of friends and relations engaged in that massive and hazardous operation; of the subsequent ebb and flow of the battles in France and then in Germany itself; and of the gradual realisation that the war really was at least coming to an end.

Since those D-Day commemorations, Prince Philip and I have been to Russia. While we were in St. Petersburg, we had the opportunity to honour the millions of patriotic Russians who died fighting the common enemy. To see British and Russian veterans standing together, in memor`of the sacrifices of their comrades-in-arms, was a moving experience. I never thought it would be possible in my lifetime to join with the Patriarch of Moscow and his congregation in a service in that wonderful cathedral in the heart of the Moscow Kremlin. This Christmas, as we pray for peace at home and abroad – not least in Russia itself – we can also give thanks that such cathedrals and churches will be full and that the great bells, which greeted us, will beringing out to celebrate our Saviour's birth.

*What is it that makes people turn from violence, and try to bring peace to their community? Most of all, I believe, it is their determination to bring reality to their hopes for a better world for their children.*

We are frequently reminded, of course, that violence and hatred are still all too much in evidence. We can take some comfort, however, from the fact that more people throughout the world, year by year, have real hope of their children growing up in peace and free from fear. Last Christmas we were witnessing the signs of a new dawn after the long bitterness, and this year these signs have become steadily stronger. If that new dawn is to be a real and not a false one, courage, patience and faith will be sorely needed – those same qualities which kept the flame of hope alive in the war-torn countries of Europe and the Far East in the dark days of the last war.

Christ taught us to love our enemies and to do good to them that hate us. It is a hard lesson to learn, but this year we have seen shining examples of that generosity of spirit, which alone can banish division and prejudice. In Northern Ireland, peace is gradually taking root; a fully democratic South Africa has been welcomed back into the Commonwealth; and, in the Middle East, long-standing enmities are healing.
What is it that makes people turn from violence, and try to bring peace to their community? Most of all, I believe, it is their determination to bring reality to their hopes of a better world for their children. The sight of the happy faces of children and young people in Russia, in South Africa, where so much has changed with such extraordinary speed in the last year, and in Northern Ireland, where there is real hope of a permanent end to the bitterness of recent years, should be enough to convince even the most hard-hearted that peace is worth striving for.

On her historic visit to Russia, The Queen visited the Dormition Cathedral of the Moscow Kremlin. Here she emerges with the Patriarch of Moscow and All Russia, Alexy II and Russia's President, Boris Yeltsin.

The Queen and Russian President Boris Yeltsin drink a toast at a state banquet in Moscow in 1994.

Next year, we shall commemorate the fiftieth anniversary of the end of the Second World War. The celebrations will no doubt be spectacular, and I hope we all enjoy them. But we can also, each in our own way, ensure that they leave a lasting mark in history.

If we resolve to be considerate and to help our neighbours; to make friends with people of different races and religions; and, as our Lord said, to look to our own faults before we criticise others, we will be keeping faith with those who landed in Normandy and fought so doggedly for their belief in freedom, peace and human decency. The poet Siegfried Sassoon, amidst all the horrors of war, still found himself able to write these words:-

*Everyone's voice was suddenly lifted*
*And beauty came like the setting sun.*

If he could see the beauty from the trenches of Flanders surely we can look for it in our own lives, this Christmas and in the coming year. Happy Christmas and God bless you.

# 1995

*This year The Queen and her mother led national celebrations for the fiftieth anniversary of the end of World War II. The Queen also paid her first visit to South Africa since 1947 and met Nelson Mandela, five years after his release from prison. In her Christmas Broadcast The Queen reflected on the need for peace.*

During a year of wartime commemorations which has seen Commonwealth countries honouring their past, it has sometimes been tempting to let nostalgia lend a rosy glow to memories of war, and to forget the benefits of the relatively peaceful years bought for us by the heroism and sacrifice to which we have been paying tribute. Those who suffered the horrors of warfare, in whatever guise, will not have been prey to this temptation. For them, war was not a *Boy's Own* tale of comradeship and good cheer, but one of hard slog, danger, suffering and exhaustion.

Those songs we sang during the VE Day commemorations did much to brighten the days of war, and they certainly cheered us last May. But, as any veteran will tell you, there was a lot more to the war years than dreaming of the White Cliffs of Dover. In talking to the veterans, I was forcibly reminded of the detachment with which those personally unaffected by violence can view its effect on others.

This seems particularly true of Northern Ireland, where the present peace of a year and more has been welcomed by all right-thinking people here and abroad. Now, however, the 'process' is at something of a crossroads as we speculate about what happens next. But it seems to me that much of the expert analysis of the manoeuvring and negotiating is somewhat detached from the reality as seen by those whom I meet who live and work in Northern Ireland. They, who for 25 years have lived their lives in the dark and relentless shadow of the gun and the bomb, do not seem to have as much time for past history and prejudice as do those who commentate and pronounce on the situation, often from afar.

For those who have seen family, friends and neighbours die by violence, the bomb and the gun are the weapons of hatred which have blighted their lives for at least a quarter of a century: surely, they say, now is the time to lay them down: surely there can be discussion of a peaceful and prosperous future conducted without the threat of a return to the old evil ways. I echo those sentiments today. I pray that those who can exercise that threat, whoever and wherever they may be, will be persuaded that the old way was the wrong way, and that to revert to it is unthinkable.

We heard much, in May and August this year, of how the future of the free world was saved by the ordinary men and women who did their bit for the victory of 1945. It is the ordinary men and women who, so often, have done more than anyone else to bring peace to troubled lands. It is they who suffer most, and it is up to others to see that their courage and common sense are rewarded. It should not be too much to ask.

*It is the ordinary men and women who, so often have done more than anyone else to bring peace to troubled lands. It is they who suffer most, and it is up to others to see that their courage and common sense are rewarded.*

During my visit to South Africa last March, I was able to see, in a township, how the energy and inspiration of one person could benefit thousands of others. And that one person would lay no claim to be anything other than ordinary — whatever you or I might think of her!

I have of course used the Christmas story before in this context. But I cannot think of any Christmas of my reign when the message of the angels has been more apt. Think, for instance, of all the children round the world suffering from the effects of war and the unscrupulous use of power. Some of them are growing up in countries of the Commonwealth, an organisation which is proud of its devotion to the principle of good government. Those children will, however, be less impressed by communiqués and good intentions than by seeing democratically elected governments governing with justice and with honour.

'Blessed be the peacemakers', Christ said, 'for they shall be called the children of God'. It is especially to those of you, often peacemakers without knowing it, who are fearful of a troubled and uncertain future, that I bid a Happy Christmas. It is your good sense and good will which have achieved so much. It must not and will not go to waste. May there be still happier Christmases to come, for you and your children. You deserve the best of them.

Happy Christmas and God bless you all.

*Opposite above:* Among the world leaders present to hear The Queen speak at the D-Day commemorative banquet in Portsmouth Guildhall were French President Francois Mitterrand and US President Bill Clinton. *Below:* The Queen enjoys meeting veterans at the fiftieth anniversary of the Arromanches landings in Normandy.

# 1996

*In her Christmas Broadcast The Queen relected on the historic visits she made to Poland and the Czech Republic, and the visit of Nelson Mandela to London. She recalled the terrible massacres at Dunblane in Scotland, and Port Arthur, Tasmania.*

To look back is not necessarily to be nostalgic. When I come to Sandringham each year, I like to reflect on what Christmas must have been like when King Edward VII, my great-grandfather, and Queen Alexandra first came here as young parents.I remember my own childhood Christmases here, with my father and mother, and a great family gathering, and now I delight in seeing my children and grandchildren enjoying the same traditions.

Christmas is the celebration of the birth of the founder of the Christian faith, an event which took place almost 2000 years ago; every year, at this time, we are asked to look back at that extraordinary story and remind ourselves of the message which inspired Christ's followers then, and which is just as relevant today. At Christmas I enjoy looking back on some of the events of the year. Many have their roots in history but still have a real point for us today. I recall, especially, a dazzling spring day in Norwich when I attended the Maundy Service, the Cathedral providing a spectacular setting. The lovely service is always a reminder of Christ's words to his disciples: 'Love one another; as I have loved you.' It sounds so simple yet it proves so hard to obey.

In June came the Trooping the Colour, a vivid reminder of this country's proud military tradition, and of the discipline and dedication that our servicemen and women show in their taxing tasks of peace-keeping in many distant parts of the world. Then, in October, I opened Parliament. This is not just a State occasion, but also a symbol of the process of parliamentary democracy that we enjoy here in Britain, and in so many countries of the Commonwealth. It is a process which seeks to express the ideal of the equality of all citizens under the law.

So, the past, with its traditions, has its lessons for us in 1996. And this year, in our travels, Prince Philip and I have also been looking to the future. I and all my family have always felt that one of our most important duties is to express, in our visits overseas, the goodwill of our country towards friends abroad, near and far. So, last spring, we visited Poland and the Czech Republic, where we saw the development of democracy and prosperity in countries which only recently were communist-governed. And everywhere we received the best of welcomes. In the autumn we

went to Thailand, where we renewed old friendships and witnessed the blending of tradition with a dynamic commercial spirit.

There was also a happy visit to this country by the President of France. And I shall never forget the state visit of President Mandela. The most gracious of men has shown us all how to accept the facts of the past without bitterness, how to see new opportunities as more important than old disputes and how to look forward with courage and optimism. His example is a continuing inspiration to the whole Commonwealth and to all those everywhere who work for peace and reconciliation.

This, I know, has been a difficult year for many families. Discord, sickness, bereavement, even tragedy have touched all too many lives. We recall, with sadness and bewilderment, the horror of Dunblane and Port Arthur. We watch anxiously as violence threatens again to disrupt the lives of the people of Northern Ireland. In difficult times, it is tempting for all of us, especially those who suffer, to look back and say 'if only'. But to look back in that way is to look down a blind alley. Better to look forward and say 'if only'.

If only we can live up to the example of the child who was born at Christmas with a love that came to embrace the whole world. If only we can let him recapture for us that time when we faced the future with childhood's unbounded faith. Armed with that faith, the New Year, with all its challenges and chances, should hold no terrors for us, and we should be able to embark upon it undaunted. My family joins me in wishing each one of you a very Happy Christmas.

In the previous year, The Queen had been welcomed to South Africa by new President Mandela, just five years after he had been released from prison. The two struck up a warm relationship and Mandela paid a return state visit to London in 1996.

# 1997

*This year was marked by the tragic death of Diana, Princess of Wales and a huge outpouring of public grief. In marked contrast, The Queen and Prince Philip celebrated their Golden Wedding anniversary at service in Westminster Abbey.*

At the Christian heart of this United Kingdom stands Westminster Abbey, and it was right that it provided the setting for two events this year – one of them almost unbearably sad, and one, for Prince Philip and me, tremendously happy. Joy and sadness are part of all our lives. Indeed, the poet William Blake tells us that:

> *Joy and woe are woven fine,*
> *A clothing for the soul divine,*
> *Under every grief and pine*
> *Runs a joy with silken twine.*

This interweaving of joy and woe has been very much brought home to me and my family during the last months. We all felt the shock and sorrow of Diana's death. Thousands upon thousands of you expressed your grief most poignantly in the wonderful flowers and messages left in tribute to her. That was a great comfort to all those close to her, while people all around the world joined us here in Britain for that service in Westminster Abbey.

But Prince Philip and I also knew the joy of our Golden Wedding. We were glad to be able to share this joy at Buckingham Palace with many other couples, who are celebrating their fiftieth anniversary this year. Then, on our own anniversary day, came a very different service at Westminster Abbey, this time the 'silken twine' a service of thanksgiving for our fifty happy years together. After that service we had a chance to meet and chat to so many different people.

I will never forget that day, nor a day five years ago when Windsor Castle suffered a terrible fire. More than a hundred rooms were badly damaged. But out of the disaster

The Queen looks some of the many thousands of bouquets left at both Kensington and Buckingham Palaces after the death of Diana, Princess of Wales. On returning from Balmoral, The Queen made an impromptu stop at the palace gate and talked to members of the waiting public.

came opportunities for all sorts of people to display their range of skills, their love of history, and their faith in the future. Last month the restoration of the Castle was completed and it is shortly to be open again for all to see. It is a mixture of the original with later additions and alterations – and, the result, a vigorous blend of the old and the new.

And so it has been in the Commonwealth. Prince Philip and I were touched by the way the Canadian people welcomed us again to Canada. We were delighted to be invited to Pakistan and India on the fiftieth anniversary of their Independence, and to celebrate their achievements since 1947.

The Prince of Wales represented Britain when the people of Hong Kong marked their return to China – in spectacular fashion. Many of you might have felt a twinge of sadness as we in Britain bade them farewell, but we should be proud of the success of our partnership in Hong Kong and in how peacefully the old Empire has been laid to rest.

Out of the old Empire sprang the Commonwealth family of nations that we know today, and that, too, has grown and changed over the years.In October, fifty-one representatives of Commonwealth governments met in Edinburgh, very much in the spirit of a family gathering. We all enjoy meeting old friends and making new ones, but there was also important business to be done. The world saw that the Commonwealth can make a major contribution to international relations and prosperity.

The meeting also showed that unity and diversity can go hand in hand. Recent developments at home, which have allowed Scotland and Wales greater say in the way they are governed, should be seen in that light and as proof that the kingdom can still enjoy all the benefits of remaining united.Being united – that is, feeling a unity of purpose – is the glue that bonds together the members of a family, a country, a Commonwealth. Without it, the parts are only fragments of a whole; with it, we can be much more than the sum of those fragments.

For most of us this is a happy family day. But I am well aware that there are many of you who are alone, bereaved, or suffering. My heart goes out to you, and I pray that we, the more fortunate ones, can unite to lend a helping hand whenever it is needed, and not 'pass by on the other side'.

St Paul spoke of the first Christmas as the kindness of God dawning upon the world. The world needs that kindness now more than ever – the kindness and consideration for others that disarms malice and allows us to get on with one another with respect and affection. Christmas reassures us that God is with us today. But, as I have discovered afresh for myself this year, he is always present in the kindness shown by our neighbours and the love of our friends and family.

God bless you all and Happy Christmas.

*Opposite above:* The Queen and Prince Philip arrive at Guildhall for an event celebrating their Golden Wedding Anniversary; *Opposite below:* The Golden Wedding Anniversary garden party at Buckingham Palace on 15 July included 4000 guests, all couples celebrating fifty years of marriage.

# 20 November 1997
# Golden Wedding Anniversary

*After fifty years of marriage, The Queen made this memorable speech at a lunch in The Banqueting House, London. She reflected on the changes she had seen, before paying an unprecedented public tribute to her husband.*

When Prince Philip and I were married on this day fifty years ago, Britain had just endured six years of war, emerging battered but victorious. Prince Philip had served in the Royal Navy in the Far East, while I was grappling, in the ATS, with the complexities of the combustion engine and learning to drive an ambulance with care.

Today, Prime Minister, we accept your generous hospitality in a very different Britain. The Cold War is over and our country is at peace. The economy in your charge, and which you inherited, is soundly based and growing. And, during these last fifty years, the mass-media culture has transformed our lives in any number of ways, allowing us to learn more about our fellow human beings than, in 1947, we would have thought possible.

What a remarkable fifty years they have been: for the world, for the Commonwealth and for Britain. Think what we would have missed if we had never heard the Beatles or seen Margot Fonteyn dance: never have watched television, used a mobile telephone or surfed the Net (or, to be honest, listened to other people talking about surfing the Net). We would never have heard someone speak from the Moon: never have watched England win the World Cup or Red Rum three Grand Nationals. We would never have heard that Everest had been scaled, DNA unravelled, the Channel tunnel built, hip replacements become commonplace. Above all, speaking personally, we would never have known the joys of having children and grandchildren.

As you say Prime Minister, since I came to the throne in 1952, ten Prime Ministers have served the British people and have come to see me each week at Buckingham Palace. The first, Winston Churchill, had charged with the cavalry at Omdurman. You, Prime Minister, were born in the year of my Coronation.

You have all had, however, one thing in common. Your advice to me has been invaluable, as has that from your counterparts, past and present, in the other countries of which I am Queen. I have listened carefully to it all. I say, most sincerely, that I could not have done my job without it. For I know that, despite the huge constitutional difference between a hereditary monarchy and an elected government, in reality the gulf is not so wide. They are complementary institutions, each with its own role to play. And each, in its different way, exists only with the support and consent of the people. That consent, or the lack of it, is expressed for you, Prime Minister, through the ballot box. It is a tough, even brutal, system but at least the message is a clear one for all to read.

For us, a Royal Family, however, the message is often harder to read, obscured as it can be by deference, rhetoric or the conflicting currents of public opinion. But read it we must. I have done my best, with Prince Philip's constant love and help, to interpret it correctly through the years of our marriage and of my reign as your Queen. And we shall, as a family, try together to do so in the future.

It often falls to the Prime Minister, and the Government of the day, to be the bearer of the messages sent from people to Sovereign. Prime Minister, I know that you, like your predecessors, will always pass such messages, as you read them, without fear or favour. I shall value that, and am grateful for your assurances of the loyalty and support of your Government in years to come. I wish you wisdom and God's help in your determination that Britain should remain a country to be proud of. And, as one working couple to another, Prince Philip and I hope that on 29 March 2030 you and your wife will be celebrating your own Golden Wedding.

And talking of the future, I believe that there is an air of confidence in this country of ours just now. I pray that we, people, Government and Royal Family, for we are one, can prove it to be justified and that Britain will enter the next millennium, glad, confident and a truly United Kingdom.

This, too, is an opportunity for Prince Philip and me to offer, in the words of one of the most beautiful prayers in the English language, our 'humble and hearty thanks' to all those in Britain and around the world who have welcomed us and sustained us and our family, in the good times and the bad, so unstintingly over many years. This has given us strength, most recently during the sad days after the tragedy of Diana's death. It is you, if I may now speak to all of you directly, who have seen us through, and helped us to make our duty fun. We are deeply grateful to you, each and every one.

Yesterday I listened as Prince Philip spoke at the Guildhall, and I then proposed our host's health. Today the roles are reversed. All too often, I fear, Prince Philip has had to listen to me speaking. Frequently we have discussed my intended speech beforehand and, as you will imagine, his views have been expressed in a forthright manner. He is someone who doesn't take easily to compliments but he has, quite simply, been my strength and stay all these years, and I, and his whole family, and this and many other countries, owe him a debt greater than he would ever claim, or we shall ever know. Prime Minister, thank you for helping us to celebrate a very special day in our lives.

# 1998

*This year The Queen's Christmas Broadcast focused on the lessons to be learnt by each generation from each other. It included film of Queen Elizabeth the Queen Mother visiting the Field of Remembrance at Westminster Abbey, The Queen at Ypres and in Paris and the reception for the Prince of Wales's fiftieth birthday.*

Christmas is a time for reflection and renewal. For Christians the year's end has a special and familiar significance, but all faiths have their calendars, their sign-posts, which ask us to pause from time to time and think further than the hectic daily round. We do that as individuals, with our families, and as members of our local communities.

It is not always easy for those in their teens or twenties to believe that someone of my age — of the older generation — might have something useful to say to them. But I would say that my mother has much to say to me. Indeed, her vigour and enjoyment of life is a great example of how to close the so-called generation gap. She has an extraordinary capacity to bring happiness into other people's lives. And her own vitality and warmth is returned to her by those whom she meets.

But there are many of my mother's generation still with us. They can remember the First World War. Prince Philip and I can recall only the Second. I know that those memories of ours define us as old, but they are shared with millions of others, in Britain and the Commonwealth, people who often feel forgotten by the march of time. They remember struggles unknown to young people today, and which they will not forget. Nor should their countries forget them. Memories such as these are a consequence of age, and not a virtue in themselves. But with age does come experience and that can be a virtue if it is sensibly used. Though we each lead different lives, the experience of growing older, and the joys and emotions which it brings, are familiar to us all.

It is hard to believe that a half century has passed since our son Charles was christened, and now, last month, he has celebrated his fiftieth birthday. It was a moment of great happiness and pride on our part in all he has achieved during the last three decades.

As a daughter, a mother and a grandmother, I often find myself seeking advice, or being asked for it, in all three capacities. No age group has a monopoly of wisdom, and indeed I think the young can sometimes be wiser than us. But the older I get, the more conscious I become of the difficulties young people have to face as they learn to live in the modern world. We parents and grandparents must learn to trust our

The Queen attends a Garter Ceremony at St George's Chapel, Windsor. This ancient ceremony, which takes place every June, dates back to the reign of Edward III, who set up a group of knights, called the Order of the Garter. Today the Knights, both male and female are chosen for their public service.

*As a daughter, mother and grandmother I often find myself seeking advice, or being asked for it. No age group has a monopoly of wisdom ... I think that the young can sometimes be wiser than us.*

children and grandchildren as they seize their opportunities, but we can, at the same time, caution and comfort if things go wrong, or guide and explain if we are needed.

My own grandchildren and their generation have a remarkable grasp of modern technology. They are lucky to have the freedom to travel and learn about foreign cultures at an age when the appetite for learning is keen. I see them pushing out the boundaries of science, sport and music, of drama and discovery. Last June Prince Philip and I gave a party for 900 of Britain's Young Achievers. Buckingham Palace was brimming with young people who, in their short lives, have already set an example to us all: they are living proof that the timeless virtues of honesty, integrity, initiative and compassion are just as important today as they have ever been.

We hear much of 'public life' — the hurly-burly of Parliament, the media, big business, city life. But for most people their contribution, at whatever age, is made quietly through their local communities just like so many of those Young Achievers. To most of them, service is its own reward. Their 'public life' is their church, their school, their sports club, their local council. My work, and the work of my family, takes us every week into that quiet sort of 'public life', where millions of people give their time, unpaid and usually unsung, to the community, and indeed to those most at risk of exclusion from it.

We see these volunteers at work in organisations such as the Scouts and Guides, the Cadet Force, the Red Cross and St. John's, The Duke of Edinburgh's Award Scheme and The Prince's Trust.These organisations, and those who serve them so selflessly, provide the bridges across which the generations travel, meet and learn from one another. They give us, with our families, our sense of belonging.

It is they that help define our sense of duty. It is they that can make us strong as individuals, and keep the nation's heartbeat strong and steady too. Christmas is a good time for us to recognise all that they do for us and to say a heartfelt thank you to each and every one of them. Happy Christmas to you all.

*Opposite:* During a visit to the Castlemilk area of Glasgow, The Queen was invited to tea with local resident Mrs Susan McCarron and her ten your old son James.

# 1999

*This year's Broadcast looked forward to the start of a new century and a new millennium. The Queen also chose to remind us of the lessons of history. The Broadcast featured a reception for young achievers at the Palace of Holyroodhouse.*

Avery Happy Christmas to you all. Listening to the choir from St. George's Chapel, Windsor, reminds me that this season of carols and Christmas trees is a time to take stock; a time to reflect on the events of the past year and to make resolutions for the new year ahead.

This December we are looking back not just on one year, but on a hundred years and a thousand years. History is measured in centuries. More than ever we are aware of being a tiny part of the infinite sweep of time when we move from one century and one millennium to another. And as I look to the future I have no doubt at all that the one certainty is change – and the pace of that change will only seem to increase.

The Queen with Flight Lieutenant Jerry Rawlings, President of Ghana, during a durbar (ceremonial gathering) of chiefs during a visit to Accra, Ghana.

This is true for all of us – young and old. On my mother's ninety-ninth birthday last August I was struck by how the inevitability of change affects us all, and how different were my mother's early years compared with those of my grandchildren. For many of their generation the future is a source of excitement, hope and challenge.

For others however the future is a cause of understandable anxiety. There are many, for example, of my age or amongst the more vulnerable in society who worry that they will be left behind. The sheer rate of change seems to be sweeping away so much that is familiar and comforting.But I do not think that we should be over-anxious. We can make sense of the future – if we understand the lessons of the past. Winston

Churchill, my first Prime Minister, said that 'the further backward you look, the further forward you can see'.

It was this importance of history which was much on my mind when I opened the new Scottish Parliament in July this year. Devolution in Scotland and Wales, and more recently the very welcome progress in Northern Ireland, are responses to today's changed circumstances, but they need to be seen in their historical contexts. History and a common past have also played an important part in bringing together so many different nations into the modern Commonwealth. This was a frequent theme last month at the Commonwealth conference in South Africa. At that meeting many of us highlighted the way in which the varied strands of our shared history have been woven together so that we can more effectively address the challenges and opportunities ahead.

The Commonwealth, as with the process of devolution in the United Kingdom, reminds us of the importance of bringing the lessons of the past to bear on the aspirations for a better future. To do this we need to draw from our history those constant and unchanging values which have stood the test of time and experience. Fairness and compassion, justice and tolerance; these are the landmarks from the past which can guide us through the years ahead. These timeless values tell us above all about the way we should relate to people rather than to things; thinking of others, not just of ourselves.

Earlier this autumn in Manchester I visited some of the emergency services, whose responsibilities day in and day out are based on concern for others. As always they are on duty over these Christmas and New Year holidays. Up and down the country people like those firemen, nurses and ambulancemen I met are working tirelessly to help others. They remind us of the responsibility of each and every one of us to show concern for our neighbours and those less fortunate than ourselves. I believe that this provides us with the direction and resolve required for the years ahead.

The future is not only about new gadgets, modern technology or the latest fashion, important as these may be. At the centre of our lives – today and tomorrow – must be the message of caring for others, the message at the heart of Christianity and of all the great religions.

This message – love thy neighbour as thyself – may be for Christians 2,000 years old. But it is as relevant today as it ever was. I believe it gives us the guidance and the reassurance we need as we step over the threshold into the twenty-first century. And I for one am looking forward to this new Millennium. May I wish you all a Merry Christmas and, in this year of all years, a very Happy New Year.

# 2000

*The Queen used her Christmas Broadcast at the end of the year to reflect on the true start of the new Millennium and the role of faith in communities. The broadcast included film of that year's visit to Australia.*

By any measure this Millennium year has been an unforgettable one. Since the turn of the year it has been celebrated and marked in this country and throughout the Commonwealth, and it has been a particular pleasure for me to visit Millennium projects large and small, which will be reminders for generations to come of the time when the twenty-first century began.

But as this year draws to a close I would like to reflect more directly and more personally on what lies behind all the celebrations of these past twelve months.

Christmas is the traditional, if not the actual, birthday of a man who was destined to change the course of our history. And today we are celebrating the fact that Jesus Christ was born two thousand years ago; this is the true Millennium anniversary. The simple facts of Jesus' life give us little clue as to the influence he was to have on the world. As a boy he learnt his father's trade as a carpenter. He then became a preacher, recruiting twelve supporters to help him.But his ministry only lasted a few years and he himself never wrote anything down. In his early thirties he was arrested, tortured and crucified with two criminals. His death might have been the end of the story, but then came the resurrection and with it the foundation of the Christian faith.

Even in our very material age the impact of Christ's life is all around us. If you want to see an expression of Christian faith you have only to look at our awe-inspiring cathedrals and abbeys, listen to their music, or look at their stained glass windows, their books and their pictures. But the true measure of Christ's influence is not only in the lives of the saints but also in the good works quietly done by millions of men and women day in and day out throughout the centuries.

Many will have been inspired by Jesus' simple but powerful teaching: love God and love thy neighbour as thyself – in other words, treat others as you would like them to treat you. His great emphasis was to give spirituality a practical purpose.

The splendidly rugged Millenium Monument in Guernsey, Channel Islands is 'unveiled' by The Queen in July 2000.

*The Bible, the Koran and the sacred texts of the Jews and Hindus, Buddhists and Sikhs, are all sources of divine inspiration and practical guidance passed down through the generations.*

Whether we believe in God or not, I think most of us have a sense of the spiritual, that recognition of a deeper meaning and purpose in our lives, and I believe that this sense flourishes despite the pressures of our world. This spirituality can be seen in the teachings of other great faiths. Of course religion can be divisive, but the Bible, the Koran and the sacred texts of the Jews and Hindus, Buddhists and Sikhs, are all sources of divine inspiration and practical guidance passed down through the generations.

To many of us our beliefs are of fundamental importance. For me the teachings of Christ and my own personal accountability before God provide a framework in which I try to lead my life. I, like so many of you, have drawn great comfort in difficult times from Christ's words and example.

I believe that the Christian message, in the words of a familiar blessing, remains profoundly important to us all:

> *Go forth into the world in peace,*
> *be of good courage,*
> *hold fast that which is good,*
> *render to no man evil for evil,*
> *strengthen the faint-hearted,*
> *support the weak,*
> *help the afflicted,*
> *honour all men.*

It is a simple message of compassion... and yet as powerful as ever today, two thousand years after Christ's birth. I hope this day will be as special for you as it is for me. May I wish you all a very Happy Christmas.

*Opposite above:* The Guard Commander of the Australian Federation Guard presents his sword before The Queen inspects the guard at Government House, Canberra in March; *Opposite below:* The residents of the outback town of Bourke, 900km northwest of Sydney, give The Queen an enthusiastic welcome during her sixteen-day tour.

# 20 March 2000
# Sydney Opera House

*This was The Queen's first visit to Australia since voters decided to retain her as Head of State. In this speech she expressed her pleasure at the referendum result and reaffirmed her continuing dedication to the nation.*

I am delighted to be back in Australia after eight years. I can think of no better way to begin this two-week visit this morning than at the Sydney Opera House, recognised and acknowledged everywhere as a symbol of Australia's determination to make its mark in the world as such a lively, distinctive and innovative nation.

I am grateful to those of you who have come here today for this lunch. Prince Philip and I have over the years deeply appreciated the warmth and generosity shown to us by Australians in every corner of the world...

We are starting the programme in the big cities, but I am glad that our tour this year includes a number of rural and regional areas. We are particularly looking forward to meeting people from these more remote locations who for generations have been such a distinct and enduring part of the Australian way of life.

This is my thirteenth visit to Australia and I have seen the Australian economy change and develop dramatically since those early days of the 1950s.Compared to some of those earlier tours the nation is enjoying a new era of prosperity. Australia has weathered the Asian financial crisis that afflicted so many of its neighbours and now has one of the fastest-growing economies in the developed world...I know that the fairness and decency for which this country is rightly renowned will mean that continued efforts are made to ensure that this prosperity touches all Australians.

It remains a sad fact of life that many indigenous Australians face a legacy of economic and social disadvantage. Others, particularly from some rural areas, feel left behind. The country's response in trying to find ways of helping all Australians to share in the country's growing wealth will require patience, determination and goodwill from all members of the community.

As we look back over the last year it has also been one of extraordinary Australian sporting achievement. 'Advance Australia Fair' was played on the sports fields of the world more often in 1999 than perhaps any other year.

It was a great personal pleasure to present the Rugby World Cup to John Eales in Cardiff in November last year, which complemented Australian successes in so many other men's and women's sports - from cricket to tennis, from netball to hockey and even, I am told, to aerial freestyle skiing. This extraordinary run of national success says much about the Australian character.

Since I was last here, Australia has also enhanced its reputation as an active and responsible partner in world affairs. As Head of the Commonwealth may I pay tribute to the energetic role which Australia continues to play in that organisation....

In January next year Australia will mark the centenary of Federation and one hundred years of nationhood. It will be a time of justified celebration, but I hope it will also be a time of pause and quiet reflection.

At that time I shall reflect – perhaps with that hint of surprise which comes with age – that my formal commitment to Australia will have spanned almost precisely half of this country's life as a federated nation. You can understand therefore that it was with the closest interest that I followed the debate leading up to the referendum held last year on the proposal to amend the Constitution.

I have always made it clear that the future of the monarchy in Australia is an issue for you, the Australian people, and you alone to decide by democratic and constitutional means. It should not be otherwise. As I said at the time, I respect and accept the outcome of the referendum. In the light of the result last November, I shall continue faithfully to serve as Queen of Australia under the Constitution to the very best of my ability, as I have tried to do for these past forty-eight years. It is my duty to seek to remain true to the interests of Australia and all Australians as we enter the twenty-first century.

That is my duty. It is also my privilege and my pleasure. I cannot forget that I was on my way to Australia when my father died. Since then and since I first stepped ashore here in Sydney in February 1954 I have felt part of this rugged, honest, creative land. I have shared in the joys and the sorrows, the challenges and the changes that have shaped this country's history over these past fifty years.

But we must look forward as well as back. Australia has always been a country on the move and will go on being so - it is not for nothing that the anthem is 'Advance Australia Fair'.

Whatever the future may bring, my lasting respect and deep affection for Australia and Australians everywhere will remain as strong as ever. That is what I have come here to say; that is why I am pleased to be back; and that is why I am looking forward to these next two weeks amongst you in this great country.

# 2001

*This year saw large-scale terrorist attacks on New York and Washington, in which around 3,000 people died; an outbreak of foot-and-mouth disease in the UK's farming community, and famine in Sudan. In her Broadcast, The Queen stressed the importance of communities working together.*

For many people all over the world, the year 2001 seems to have brought them more than their fair share of trials and disasters. There have been storms and droughts as well as epidemics and famine. And this country has not been spared, with the floods this time last year, and foot-and-mouth disease, which has had such devastating consequences for our farmers and rural communities.

They and others whose livelihoods have been affected continue to suffer hardship and anxiety long after the newspaper headlines have moved on. But whilst many of these events were of natural origin, it was the human conflicts and the wanton acts of crime and terror against fellow human beings which have so appalled us all.

The terrorist outrages in the United States last September brought home to us the pain and grief of ordinary people the world over who find themselves innocently caught up in such evil. During the following days we struggled to find ways of expressing our horror at what had happened. As so often in our lives at times of tragedy – just as on occasions of celebration and thanksgiving – we look to the Church to bring us together as a nation or as a community in commemoration and tribute.

It is to the Church that we turn to give meaning to these moments of intense human experience through prayer, symbol and ceremony. In these circumstances so many of us, whatever our religion, need our faith more than ever to sustain and guide us. Every one of us needs to believe in the value of all that is good and honest; we need to let this belief drive and influence our actions.

All the major faiths tell us to give support and hope to others in distress. We in this country have tried to bring comfort to all those who were bereaved, or who suffered loss or injury in September's tragic events through those moving services at St Paul's and more recently at Westminster Abbey. On these occasions and during the countless other acts of worship during this past year, we came together as a community – of relations, friends and neighbours – to draw strength in troubled times from those around us.

I believe that strong and open communities matter both in good times as well as bad.

Certainly they provide a way of helping one another. I would like to pay tribute to so many of you who work selflessly for others in your neighbourhood needing care and support. Communities also give us an important sense of belonging, which is a compelling need in all of us. We all enjoy moments of great happiness and suffer times of profound sadness; the happiness is heightened, the sadness softened when it is shared.

But there is more than that. A sense of belonging to a group, which has in common the same desire for a fair and ordered society, helps to overcome differences and misunderstanding by reducing prejudice, ignorance and fear.

We all have something to learn from one another, whatever our faith — be it Christian or Jewish, Muslim, Buddhist, Hindu or Sikh — whatever our background, whether we be young or old, from town or countryside. This is an important lesson for us all during this festive season. For Christmas marks a moment to pause, to reflect and believe in the possibilities of rebirth and renewal. Christ's birth in Bethlehem so long ago remains a powerful symbol of hope for a better future. After all the tribulations of this year, this is surely more relevant than ever. As we come together amongst family and friends and look forward to the coming year, I hope that in the months to come we shall be able to find ways of strengthening our own communities as a sure support and comfort to us all — whatever may lie ahead.

May I, in this my fiftieth Christmas message to you, once again wish every one of you a very happy Christmas.

The Queen leaves St Paul's Cathedral in London on 14 September, after attending a service of those killed in the 9/11 terrorist attacks on New York and Washington.

# 2002 ~ 2011

## HEIRS
*to the*
## THRONE

Three generations of the Royal Family before a dinner in
June 2003 at Clarence House, London to celebrate the
fiftieth anniversary of The Queen's coronation.

The Queen lost her sister, Princess Margaret, and her mother, Queen Elizabeth, The Queen Mother, within two months of each other in 2002, on 9 February and 30 March respectively. The Queen Mother was aged 101.

As others too have found, being the undercard to a monarch and to an elder sister is not an easy role to fulfil. Princess Margaret lived life to the full. Although she found many aspects of her royal life frustrating, the vivacious, attractive Princess was a breath of fresh air to the public perception of the Royal Family. In her later life, though, sadly, her hedonistic lifestyle caught up with her.

Princess Margaret had not remarried after her divorce from Lord Snowden and had been unwell for her final three years, so a private funeral was held for family only. By contrast, more than 200,000 people went to pay their respects to The Queen Mother as she lay in state in Westminster Hall, inside Parliament, over three days. For her funeral, over a million people lined the route from Westminster Abbey to St George's Chapel, Windsor Castle.

In 2002, The Queen celebrated her Golden Jubilee – the fiftieth anniversary of her accession to the throne. Prime Minister Blair began the celebrations on Monday, 29 April with a dinner for The Queen at 10 Downing Street, attended by all the former prime ministers still living. The next day, The Queen addressed both Houses of Parliament, focusing on her pride about the nation's continuing fairness and tolerance:

*These enduring British traditions and values – moderation, openness, tolerance, service – have stood the test of time, and I am convinced they will stand us in good stead in the future.*

The Queen also used this speech to launch The Queen's Golden Jubilee Annual Award for Voluntary Service by groups in the community – an award that continues to be given to this day. And just as for her twenty-fifth anniversary, she again celebrated by travelling the length and breadth of the United Kingdom as well as select countries within the Commonwealth.

As part of the ominous promise President George W. Bush made to the American people following 9/11, his 'war on terrorism' began in earnest in 2003 with the invasion of Iraq. The claim made by Prime Minister Blair and others, that Saddam Hussein would be able to assemble weapons of mass destruction within forty-five minutes, went against the official advice of the UN's Monitoring, Verification and Inspection Commission in charge of monitoring Iraq.

On 18 March 2003, fearing imminent attack, a Parliamentary proposal to wait for the United Nations' approval before declaring war was defeated by 396-217 votes and when the main motion to approve the invasion of Iraq was put forward at 10 p.m. that same day, it was won by 412-149 with 94 abstentions. There were anti-war demonstrations war in many cities worldwide; in central London the streets echoed to chants of 'Not in my name', as huge crowds marched in a passionate, but ultimately futile attempt to prevent us joining the war. British operations in Iraq lasted from 19 March 2003 to 22 May 2011. In all there were 183 fatalities. The figures for those wounded were only released after 1 January 2006 and they reached 3,598.

Saddam Hussein's government was defeated within days of the Allied Forces invasion, but Hussein himself went into hiding for nine months before being captured by US forces in December 2003. The former president was executed on 30 December 2006 by the Iraqi government for crimes against humanity.

By 2008, the world was engulfed in the biggest meltdown of banking and financial systems since the Great Depression in the 1930s. The sub-prime housing market, coupled with easy credit conditions and fraudulent underwriting practices that had become the norm largely but not exclusively in America, were the catalyst for the global meltdown. There were many casualties including the extraordinary bankruptcy of the United States' fourth-largest investment bank, Lehman Brothers, on 15 September 2008, due to its heavy investment in sub-prime mortgages.

In the UK, Northern Rock, a medium-sized bank, was highly leveraged and was forced to ask the Bank of England to bail it out of its debts on 14 September 2007. The news led to huge queues outside Northern Rock offices as desperate people tried to access their savings. In the end the bank too was nationalised in February 2008. Governments globally rushed to support the banks and legislation was enacted to protect them – sometimes too quickly. The International Monetary Fund warned on 11 October 2008 that the world's financial system was on the 'brink of systematic meltdown'. We survived, just about.

In November Barack Obama, a Democrat, became the first Black President of the United States and went on to serve two terms. His inauguration attracted over 1.8 million people in person, with vast global audiences tuning in via television and internet. He lit up the nation and the world and was awarded the Nobel Peace prize in 2009, although but he inherited and had to manage the US banking crisis.

Back in the UK, the General Election on Thursday, 6 May 2010 proved to be a missed chance by Labour that would cost them dearly. The result was that no overall party was handed control

by the electorate: Conservatives won 306 seats, Labour 258, the Lib Dems 57 with Others on 29. After five days of coalition talks the Lib Dems foolishly accepted a deal with the Conservatives.

Apple's iPod was essentially the Sony Walkman of the twenty first century. Launching the 5G hard drive portable music player, Steve Jobs, its creator, said that it put '1,000 songs in your pocket'. In 2007, Jonathan Ive CBE (he was knighted in 2012) designed the iPhone and so secured Apple's future as one of the top five tech companies. To date 2.2 billion iPhones have been sold. In 2010, following the successful launches of the iPod and iPhone, the iPad was released to consumers.

On the gaming front, Sony launched its PlayStation 2 home-video games console and then in 2004 came the first portable player, the Nintendo DS. DVDs gradually overwhelmed floppy discs and Super Mario arrived. Gaming on the internet also took off. Animation in film, especially Hollywood blockbusters, became the norm, with *Finding Nemo, Ice Age* and *Up* leading the way in both cost of production and theatre box office success.

Meanwhile, in the art world Pablo Picasso's *Boy with a Pipe* (1905) and not thought to be one of his best works, sold for an eye-watering $104m (£58m) in 2004. Three years later, Damien Hirst surprised everyone when his *Lullaby Spring* – a pill cabinet – sold at Sotheby's for $19.2m (£9.6m), the highest ever price paid for a work from a living artist.

Prince William and Catherine Middleton, were married at Westminster Abbey on 29 April 2011. The television audience in the UK peaked at 26.3 million and 72 million live streams on YouTube. The couple became known as the Duke and Duchess of Cambridge.

# 2002

*After fifty years on the throne, The Queen's Golden Jubilee was clouded by sadness as she lost both her mother and sister. In her Christmas Broadcast, she acknowledged her deep sorrow, yet also reflected on the celebrations that had taken place in the UK and across the Commonwealth.*

As I look back over these past twelve months, I know that it has been about as full a year as I can remember. But Christmas itself still remains a time for reflection and a focus of hope for the future. All great religions have such times of renewal, moments to take stock before moving on to face the challenges that lie ahead.

Many of you will know only too well from your own experience, the grief that follows the death of a much-loved mother or sister. Mine were very much part of my life and always gave me their support and encouragement. But my own sadness was tempered by the generous tributes that so many of you paid to the service they gave to this country and the wider Commonwealth. At such a difficult time this gave me great comfort and inspiration as I faced up both to my own personal loss and to the busy Jubilee summer ahead.

Anniversaries are important events in all our lives. Christmas is the anniversary of the birth of Christ over two thousand years ago, but it is much more than that. It is the celebration of the birth of an idea and an ideal. In a different way I felt that the Golden Jubilee was more than just an anniversary. The celebrations were joyous occasions, but they also seemed to evoke something more lasting and profound – a sense of belonging and pride in country, town, or community; a sense of sharing a common heritage enriched by the cultural, ethnic and religious diversity of our twenty-first century society.

I hope it also provided an occasion to acknowledge the progress of the past fifty years and the contributions of those who have done so much to make this country what it is today – their leadership and example, their achievements in science, the arts and many other fields.

These celebrations also gave opportunities to recognise the valuable work undertaken by so many people in service of their communities. It was a time to remind ourselves, as the Christmas story does every year, that we must never forget the plight of the disadvantaged and excluded, that we must respond to the needs of those who may be in distress or despair. Our modern world places such heavy demands on our time

and attention that the need to remember our responsibilities to others is greater than ever. It is often difficult to keep this sense of perspective through the ups and downs of everyday life – as this year has constantly reminded me.

I know just how much I rely on my own faith to guide me through the good times and the bad. Each day is a new beginning, I know that the only way to live my life is to try to do what is right, to take the long view, to give of my best in all that the day brings, and to put my trust in God. Like others of you who draw inspiration from your own faith, I draw strength from the message of hope in the Christian gospel.

Fortified by this and the support you have given throughout the last twelve months which has meant so much to me, I look forward to the New Year, to facing the challenges and opportunities that lie ahead, and to continuing to serve you to the very best of my ability each and every day. A Happy Christmas to you all.

The death of The Queen's younger sister Princess Margaret robbed her of one of her closest confidants. This photograph was taken in May, 1988.

# 8 APRIL 2002
# THE QUEEN MOTHER

*Just weeks after the death of her sister Princess Margaret, The Queen suffered the loss her beloved mother. In her broadcast to the nation the grieving Queen thanked people for their support.*

Ever since my beloved mother died over a week ago I have been deeply moved by the outpouring of affection which has accompanied her death. My family and I always knew what she meant for the people of this country and the special place she occupied in the hearts of so many here, in the Commonwealth and in other parts of the world. But the extent of the tribute that huge numbers of you have paid my mother in the last few days has been overwhelming. I have drawn great comfort from so many individual acts of kindness and respect.

Over the years I have met many people who have had to cope with family loss, sometimes in the most tragic of circumstances. So I count myself fortunate that my mother was blessed with a long and happy life. She had an infectious zest for living, and this remained with her until the very end. I know too that her faith was always a great strength to her.

At the ceremony tomorrow I hope that sadness will blend with a wider sense of thanksgiving, not just for her life but for the times in which she lived — a century for this country and the Commonwealth not without its trials and sorrows, but also one of extraordinary progress, full of examples of courage and service as well as fun and laughter. This is what my mother would have understood, because it was the warmth and affection of people everywhere which inspired her resolve, dedication and enthusiasm for life.

I thank you for the support you are giving me and my family as we come to terms with her death and the void she has left in our midst. I thank you also from my heart for the love you gave her during her life and the honour you now give her in death. May God bless you all.

*Opposite above:* In May 1995, the Queen Mother , with the Queen and Princess Margaret, celebrates the 50th anniversary; *Opposite below:* The Queen helps her mother with some of the many bouquets she received from crowds during her ninetieth birthday celebrations in 1990.

# 2003

*The Queen's Christmas Broadcast was recorded entirely at Combermere Barracks in Windsor, the first time an outdoor location was used. The Queen reminded us of the British servicemen and women stationed in Iraq, far from their families and loved ones.*

I am sure that most of you will be celebrating Christmas at home in the company of your families and friends, but I know that some of you will not be so lucky.

This year I am speaking to you from the Household Cavalry Barracks in Windsor because I want to draw attention to the many servicemen and women who are stationed far from home this Christmas. I am thinking about their wives and children, and about their parents and friends. Separation at this time is especially hard to bear.

It is not just a matter of separation. The men and women of the Services continue to face serious risks and dangers as they carry out their duties. They have done this brilliantly. I think we all have very good reasons for feeling proud of their achievements – both in war, and as they help to build a lasting peace in trouble spots across the globe.

None of this can be achieved without paying a price. I know that all our thoughts at this time are with the families who are suffering the pain of bereavement. All those who have recently lost a close relative or friend will know how difficult Christmas can be. These individual servicemen and women are our neighbours and come from our own towns and villages; from every part of the country and from every background.

The process of training within the Navy, the Army and the Air Force has moulded them together into disciplined teams. They have learnt to take responsibility and to exercise judgement and restraint in situations of acute stress and danger. They have brought great credit to themselves and to our country as a whole.

I had an opportunity recently at the Barracks to meet some of those who played their part with such distinction in the Iraq operations. I was left with a deep sense of respect and admiration for their steadfast loyalty to each other and to our nation. I believe there is a lesson for us all here. It is that each of us can achieve much more if we work together as members of a team. The Founder of the Christian Faith himself chose twelve disciples to help him in his ministry.

I was reminded of the importance of teamwork as I presented, for the first time last summer, The Queen's Awards for Voluntary Service by groups within the community. I have been struck by how often people say to me that they are receiving their award on behalf of a team and that they do not deserve to be singled out. This annual award recognises the team rather than the individual.

In this country and throughout the Commonwealth there are groups of people who are giving their time generously to make a difference to the lives of others. As we think of them, and of our servicemen and women far from home at this Christmas time, I hope we all, whatever our faith, can draw inspiration from the words of the familiar prayer:

*Teach us good Lord*
*To serve thee as thou deservest;*
*To give, and not to count the cost;*
*To fight, and not to heed the wounds;*
*To toil, and not to seek for rest;*
*To labour, and not to ask for any reward;*
*Save that of knowing that we do thy will.*

It is this knowledge that will help us all to enjoy the Festival of Christmas. A happy Christmas to you all.

The Queen meets The Archbishop of Canterbury, Rowan Williams, during her visit to St Bartholomew the Great, London's oldest parish church. Dr Williams accepted an invitation to preside at a service of prayer and dedication for the wedding of Prince Charles and Camilla Parker Bowles, which took place in 2005.

# 6 JUNE 2004
# D-DAY COMMEMORATION

*On the sixtieth anniversary of the allied invasion of Normandy, The Queen addressed, in English and French, twenty-two heads of state and government, including British Prime Minister Tony Blair and President Bush, and hundreds of veterans.*

The invasion of France in 1944 was one of the most dramatic military operations in history. It would have been difficult enough for a single nation to plan and execute such an enterprise; for a group of allies with little previous experience in co-operation, it was a major triumph.

The operation itself was a resounding success, but it was only achieved with the sacrifice of many courageous and determined allied Servicemen, including a large number of your Canadian colleagues, who landed here with you on Juno Beach.

Britain had been directly threatened by the enemy but you came across the Atlantic from the relative security of your homeland to fight for the freedom of Europe. For Canadians, involved in the fight from its earliest months, the raid on Dieppe was a tragedy but, in retrospect, the lessons learned there proved to be life-savers for many thousands when you came to land in Normandy.

Malgré la distance entre le Canada et la Normandie, les liens entre Canadiens et Français sont très étroits. Les générations futures de Canadiens de toutes origines auront raison d'être fières de l'immense contribution de l'armée et des forces navales et de l'air canadiennes pour la libération de l'Europe.

The sixtieth anniversary of the Normandy Landings is a moment for thanksgiving, and a moment of commemoration. Today we honour all those who gave their lives in this campaign, and all of you who fought in this great struggle. I know that present and future generations join me in thanking all Canadians who took part in this great venture.

On this anniversary day, I join all your countrymen and allies in saluting you, the heroes and veterans of a historic campaign.

*Opposite above:* Prince Charles greets veterans at the 4th/7th Royal Dragoon Guards memorial in Creully, Normandy in June on the eve of the sixtieth D-Day anniversary. *Opposite below:* The Queen attends a British-French ceremony at the Bayeux cemetery in Normandy to commemorate D-Day on 6 June.

# 2004

*In her Christmas Broadcast The Queen stressed the importance of religious tolerance and fighting racial discrimination. The Indian Ocean Tsunami, which killed thousands of people across south and southeast Asia on Christmas and Boxing Days, happened too late for the Queen to include in her message.*

Christmas is for most of us a time for a break from work, for family and friends, for presents, turkey and crackers. But we should not lose sight of the fact that these are traditional celebrations around a great religious festival, one of the most important in the Christian year.

Religion and culture are much in the news these days, usually as sources of difference and conflict, rather than for bringing people together. But the irony is that every religion has something to say about tolerance and respecting others. For me as a Christian one of the most important of these teachings is contained in the parable of the Good Samaritan, when Jesus answers the question 'who is my neighbour'. It is a timeless story of a victim of a mugging who was ignored by his own countrymen but helped by a foreigner – and a despised foreigner at that.

The implication drawn by Jesus is clear. Everyone is our neighbour, no matter what race, creed or colour. The need to look after a fellow human being is far more important than any cultural or religious differences. Most of us have learned to acknowledge and respect the ways of other cultures and religions, but what matters even more is the way in which those from different backgrounds behave towards each other in everyday life.

It is vitally important that we all should participate and cooperate for the sake of the wellbeing of the whole community. We have only to look around to recognise the benefits of this positive approach in business or local government, in sport, music and the arts. There is certainly much more to be done and many challenges to be overcome. Discrimination still exists. Some people feel that their own beliefs are being threatened. Some are unhappy about unfamiliar cultures. They all need to be reassured that there is so much to be gained by reaching out to others; that diversity is indeed a strength and not a threat.

We need also to realise that peaceful and steady progress in our society of differing cultures and heritage can be threatened at any moment by the actions of extremists at home or by events abroad. We can certainly never be complacent. But there is

every reason to be hopeful about the future. I certainly recognise that much has been achieved in my lifetime. I believe tolerance and fair play remain strong British values and we have so much to build on for the future.

It was for this reason that I particularly enjoyed a story I heard the other day about an overseas visitor to Britain who said the best part of his visit had been travelling from Heathrow into Central London on the tube. His British friends were, as you can imagine, somewhat surprised, particularly as the visitor had been to some of the great attractions of the country. What do you mean? they asked.

Because, he replied, I boarded the train just as the schools were coming out. At each stop children were getting on and off – they were of every ethnic and religious background, some with scarves or turbans, some talking quietly, others playing and occasionally misbehaving together – completely at ease and trusting one another. How lucky you are, said the visitor, to live in a country where your children can grow up this way. I hope they will be allowed to enjoy this happy companionship for the rest of their lives. A Happy Christmas to you all.

The Queen attends a memorial service and meets survivors of victims of the tsunami that killed an estimated 300,000 people, including over eighty Britons, in December 2003. Members of relief agencies, family members of British victims and leaders of UK communities with close ties to the affected countries were invited to the service at St Paul's Cathedral in London, led by the Archbishop of Canterbury.

# 2005

*In 2005, following the tsunami in south east Asia, the world suffered a further series of terrible natural disasters. Then in July terrorists struck in the heart of London, killing commuters on a bus and tube trains. The Queen reflected on the year's tragedies and praised the work of those involved in providing humanitarian assistance.*

The day after my last Christmas message was broadcast, the world experienced one of the worst natural disasters ever recorded. The devastating tsunami struck countries around the Indian Ocean causing death and destruction on an unprecedented scale. This was followed by a number of vicious hurricanes across the Caribbean and the inundation of the city of New Orleans. Then in the autumn came the massive earthquake in Pakistan and India. This series of dreadful events has brought loss and suffering to so many people – and their families and friends – not only in the countries directly affected, but here in Britain and throughout the Commonwealth.

As if these disasters were not bad enough, I have sometimes thought that humanity seemed to have turned on itself – with wars, civil disturbances and acts of brutal

terrorism. In this country many people's lives were totally changed by the London bombings in July. This Christmas my thoughts are especially with those everywhere who are grieving the loss of loved ones during what for so many has been such a terrible year.

These natural and human tragedies provided the headline news; they also provoked a quite remarkable humanitarian response. People of compassion all over the world responded with immediate practical and financial help. There may be an instinct in all of us to help those in distress, but in many cases I believe this has been inspired by religious faith. Christianity is not the only religion to teach its followers to help others and to treat your neighbour as you would want to be treated yourself.

It has been clear that in the course of this year relief workers and financial support have come from members of every faith and from every corner of the world. There is no doubt that the process of rebuilding these communities is far from over and there will be fresh calls on our commitment to help in the future.

*These natural human tragedies provided the headline news; they also provided a quite remarkable humanitarian response. People of compassion all over the world responded with immediate practical and financial help.*

Certainly the need for selflessness and generosity in the face of hardship is nothing new. The veterans of the World War II whom we honoured last summer can tell us how so often, in moments of greatest trial, those around them seemed able to draw on some inner strength to find courage and compassion. We see this today in the way that young men and women are calmly serving our country around the world often in great danger.

This last year has reminded us that this world is not always an easy or a safe place to live in, but it is the only place we have. I believe also that it has shown us all how our faith – whatever our religion – can inspire us to work together in friendship and peace for the sake of our own and future generations.

For Christians this festival of Christmas is the time to remember the birth of the one we call 'the Prince of Peace' and our source of 'light and life' in both good times and bad. It is not always easy to accept his teaching, but I have no doubt that the New Year will be all the better if we do but try.

I hope you will all have a very happy Christmas this year and that you go into the New Year with renewed hope and confidence.

The Queen talks to Catholic nun Sister Mary Lawrence during her visit to the Royal London Hospital, a month after terrorist bombs exploded in central London, killing fifty-six people. She met also staff and several recovering victims.

# 2006

*This year The Queen focussed on the understanding between faiths and generations, and reflected on the importance of passing on wisdom to younger generations. The broadcast was filmed in Southwark Cathedral, where she met children working on a Nativity collage.*

I have lived long enough to know that things never remain quite the same for very long. One of the things that has not changed all that much for me is the celebration of Christmas. It remains a time when I try to put aside the anxieties of the moment and remember that Christ was born to bring peace and tolerance to a troubled world.

The birth of Jesus naturally turns our thoughts to all new-born children and what the future holds for them. The birth of a baby brings great happiness – but then the business of growing up begins. It is a process that starts within the protection and care of parents and other members of the family – including the older generation. As with any team, there is strength in combination: what grandparent has not wished for the best possible upbringing for their grandchildren or felt an enormous sense of pride at their achievements?

But the pressures of modern life sometimes seem to be weakening the links which have traditionally kept us together as families and communities. As children grow up and develop their own sense of confidence and independence in the ever-changing technological environment, there is always the danger of a real divide opening up between young and old, based on unfamiliarity, ignorance or misunderstanding.

It is worth bearing in mind that all of our faith communities encourage the bridging of that divide. The wisdom and experience of the great religions point to the need to nurture and guide the young, and to encourage respect for the elderly. Christ himself told his disciples to let the children come to him, and Saint Paul reminded parents to be gentle with their children, and children to appreciate their parents. The scriptures and traditions of the other faiths enshrine the same fundamental guidance. It is very easy to concentrate on the differences between the religious faiths and to forget what they have in common – people of different faiths are bound together by the need to help the younger generation to become considerate and active citizens.

And there is another cause for hope that we can do better in the future at bridging the generation gap. As older people remain more active for longer, the opportunities to look for new ways to bring young and old together are multiplying.

As I look back on these past twelve months, marked in particular for me by the very generous response to my eightieth birthday, I especially value the opportunities I have had to meet young people. I am impressed by their energy and vitality, and by their ambition to learn and to travel. It makes me wonder what contribution older people can make to help them realise their ambitions. I am reminded of a lady of about my age who was asked by an earnest, little grand-daughter the other day 'Granny, can you remember the Stone Age?' Whilst that may be going a bit far, the older generation are able to give a sense of context as well as the wisdom of experience which can be invaluable. Such advice and comfort are probably needed more often than younger people admit or older people recognise. I hope that this is something that all of us, young or old, can reflect on at this special time of year.

For Christians, Christmas marks the birth of our Saviour, but it is also a wonderful occasion to bring the generations together in a shared festival of peace, tolerance and goodwill. I wish you all a very happy Christmas together.

The Queen meets children of local schools during the filming of her broadcast in Southwark Cathedral.

# 2007

*In a year in which The Queen and Prince Philip marked their diamond wedding anniversary, her Christmas Broadcast described their joy of celebrating it with an extended family. She then turned her focus to those less fortunate, and the importance of supporting the disadvantaged, reaching out beyond family members at Christmas.*

One of the features of growing old is a heightened awareness of change. To remember what happened fifty years ago means that it is possible to appreciate what has changed in the meantime. It also makes you aware of what has remained constant. In my experience, the positive value of a happy family is one of the factors of human existence that has not changed. The immediate family of grandparents, parents and children, together with their extended family, is still the core of a thriving community. When Prince Philip and I celebrated our Diamond Wedding last month, we were much aware of the affection and support of our own family as they gathered round us for the occasion.

Now today, of course, marks the birth of Jesus Christ. Among other things, it is a reminder that it is the story of a family; but of a family in very distressed circumstances. Mary and Joseph found no room at the inn; they had to make do in a stable, and the new-born Jesus had to be laid in a manger. This was a family which had been shut out.

Perhaps it was because of this early experience that, throughout his ministry, Jesus of Nazareth reached out and made friends with people whom others ignored or despised. It was in this way that he proclaimed his belief that, in the end, we are all brothers and sisters in one human family. The Christmas story also draws attention to all those people who are on the edge of society – people who feel cut off and disadvantaged; people who, for one reason or another, are not able to enjoy the full benefits of living in a civilised and law-abiding community. For these people the modern world can seem a distant and hostile place.

It is all too easy to 'turn a blind eye', 'to pass by on the other side', and leave it to experts and professionals. All the great religious teachings of the world press home

Newly weds Princess Elizabeth and the Duke of Edinburgh in the grounds of Broadlands, home of the Earl of Mountbatten. Sixty years on, once again posing for diamond anniversary pictures at Broadlands , their love is still as obvious.

the message that everyone has a responsibility to care for the vulnerable. Fortunately, there are many groups and individuals, often unsung and unrewarded, who are dedicated to ensuring that the 'outsiders' are given a chance to be recognised and respected. However, each one of us can also help by offering a little time, a talent or a possession, and taking a share in the responsibility for the well-being of those who feel excluded. And also today I want to draw attention to another group of people who deserve our thoughts this Christmas. We have all been conscious of those who have given their lives, or who have been severely wounded, while serving with the Armed Forces in Iraq and Afghanistan. The dedication of the National Armed Forces Memorial was also an occasion to remember those who have suffered while serving in these and every other place of unrest since the end of the Second World War.

In November 2007 The Prince of Wales and the Duchess of Cornwall hosted a family dinner at Clarence House in London to celebrate the diamond wedding anniversary.

For their families, Christmas will bring back sad memories, and I pray that all of you, who are missing those who are dear to you, will find strength and comfort in your families and friends.

A familiar introduction to an annual Christmas Carol Service contains the words: 'Because this would most rejoice his heart, let us remember, in his name, the poor and the helpless, the cold, the hungry, and the oppressed; the sick and those who mourn, the lonely and the unloved.' Wherever these words find you, and in whatever circumstances, I want to wish you all a blessed Christmas.

# 2008

*This year, international financial meltdown contrasted with the hope and optimism inspired by the election of U.S. President Barack Obama. In her Christmas Broadcast, The Queen acknowledged the suffering the banking crisis had caused.*

Christmas is a time for celebration, but this year it is a more sombre occasion for many. Some of those things which could once have been taken for granted suddenly seem less certain and, naturally, give rise to feelings of insecurity.

People are touched by events which have their roots far across the world. Whether it is the global economy or violence in a distant land, the effects can be keenly felt at home. Once again, many of our service men and women are serving on operations in common cause to bring peace and security to troubled places. In this ninetieth year since the end of World War I, the last survivors recently commemorated the service and enormous sacrifice of their own generation. Their successors in theatres such as Iraq and Afghanistan are still to be found in harm's way in the service of others. For their loved ones, the worry will never cease until they are safely home. In such times as these we can all learn some lessons from the past. We might begin to see things in a new perspective. And certainly, we begin to ask ourselves where it is that we can find lasting happiness.

Over the years, those who have seemed to me to be the most happy, contented and fulfilled have always been the people who have lived the most outgoing and unselfish lives; the kind of people who are generous with their talents or their time. There are those who use their prosperity or good fortune for the benefit of others whether they number among the great philanthropists or are people who, with whatever they have, simply have a desire to help those less fortunate than themselves.

What they offer comes in the form of what can easily be recognised as service to the nation or service to the wider community. As often as not however, their unselfishness is a simply-taken-for-granted part of the life of their family or neighbourhood. They tend to have some sense that life itself is full of blessings, and is a precious gift for which we should be thankful. When life seems hard, the courageous do not lie down and accept defeat; instead, they are all the more determined to struggle for a better future.

I think we have a huge amount to learn from individuals such as these. And what I believe many of us share with them is a source of strength and peace of mind in our families and friends. Indeed, Prince Philip and I can reflect on

the blessing, comfort and support we have gained from our own family in this special year for our son, The Prince of Wales.

Sixty years ago, he was baptised here in the Music Room at Buckingham Palace. As parents and grandparents, we feel great pride in seeing our family make their own unique contributions to society. Through his charities, The Prince of Wales has worked to support young people and other causes for the benefit of the wider community, and now his sons are following in his footsteps.

At Christmas, we feel very fortunate to have our family around us. But for many of you, this Christmas will mean separation from loved ones and perhaps reflection on the memories of those no longer with us. I hope that, like me, you will be comforted by the example of Jesus of Nazareth who, often in circumstances of great adversity, managed to live an outgoing, unselfish and sacrificial life. Countless millions of people around the world continue to celebrate his birthday at Christmas, inspired by his teaching. He makes it clear that genuine human happiness and satisfaction lie more in giving than receiving; more in serving than in being served.

We can surely be grateful that, two thousand years after the birth of Jesus, so many of us are able to draw inspiration from his life and message, and to find in him a source of strength and courage. I hope that the Christmas message will encourage and sustain you too, now and in the coming year. I wish you all a very happy Christmas.

The Queen makes a speech during a banquet at Windsor Castle, held in honour of President Nicolas Sarkozy and his wife Carla Bruni-Sarkozy during his state visit. The President is seated to The Queen's right.

# 2009

*In her Christmas Broadcast this year, The Queen expressed sympathy for those who had lost loved ones in the continuing war in Afghanistan. She returned to one of her favourite themes, the Commonwealth, and admired the creativity and innovation shown by the younger members of this diverse international 'family'.*

Each year that passes seems to have its own character. Some leave us with a feeling of satisfaction, others are best forgotten. 2009 was a difficult year for many, in particular those facing the continuing effects of the economic downturn.

I am sure that we have all been affected by events in Afghanistan and saddened by the casualties suffered by our forces serving there. Our thoughts go out to their relations and friends who have shown immense dignity in the face of great personal loss. But, we can be proud of the positive contribution that our servicemen and women are making, in conjunction with our allies. Well over 13,000 soldiers from the United Kingdom, and across the Commonwealth — Canada, Australia, New Zealand and Singapore – are currently serving in Afghanistan. The debt of gratitude owed to these young men and women, and to their predecessors, is indeed profound.

It is sixty years since the Commonwealth was created and today, with more than a billion of its members under the age of twenty five, the organisation remains a strong and practical force for good. Recently I attended the Commonwealth Heads of Government Meeting in Trinidad and Tobago and heard how important the Commonwealth is to young people.

New communication technologies allow them to reach out to the wider world and share their experiences and viewpoints. For many, the practical assistance and networks of the Commonwealth can give skills, lend advice and encourage enterprise. It is inspiring to learn of some of the work being done by these young people, who bring creativity and innovation to the challenges they face. It is important to keep discussing issues that concern us all – there can be no more valuable role for our family of nations.

I have been closely associated with the Commonwealth through most of its existence. The personal and living bond I have enjoyed with leaders, and with people the world over, has always been more important in promoting our unity than symbolism alone. The Commonwealth is not an organisation with a mission. It is rather an opportunity for its people to work together to achieve practical solutions to problems.

In many aspects of our lives, whether in sport, the environment, business or culture, the Commonwealth connection remains vivid and enriching. It is, in lots of ways, the face of the future. And with continuing support and dedication, I am confident that this diverse Commonwealth of nations can strengthen the common bond that transcends politics, religion, race and economic circumstances.

We know that Christmas is a time for celebration and family reunions; but it is also a time to reflect on what confronts those less fortunate than ourselves, at home and throughout the world. Christians are taught to love their neighbours, having compassion and concern, and being ready to undertake charity and voluntary work to ease the burden of deprivation and disadvantage. We may ourselves be confronted by a bewildering array of difficulties and challenges, but we must never cease to work for a better future for ourselves and for others.

I wish you all, wherever you may be, a very happy Christmas.

The Queen delivers a speech during the opening ceremony of the Commonwealth Heads of Government meeting in Port of Spain, Trinidad and Tobago in November. Efforts to tackle global warming were high on the agenda.

# 6 JULY 2010
# UNITED NATIONS ADDRESS

*After forty years, The Queen returned to speak to the United Nations General Assembly. She shared her impressions of the great advances that she had observed, but also reminded the Members that there was much to be done in the world.*

Mr President, Secretary-General, Members of the General Assembly, I believe I was last here in 1957. Since then, I have travelled widely and met many leaders, ambassadors and statesmen from around the world. I address you today as Queen of sixteen United Nations Member States and as Head of the Commonwealth of fifty four countries. I have also witnessed great change, much of it for the better, particularly in science and technology, and in social attitudes. Remarkably, many of these sweeping advances have come about not because of governments, committee resolutions, or central directives - although all these have played a part - but instead because millions of people around the world have wanted them.

For the United Nations, these subtle yet significant changes in people's approach to leadership and power might have foreshadowed failure and demise. Instead, the United Nations has grown and prospered by responding and adapting to these shifts.But also, many important things have not changed. The aims and values which inspired the United Nations Charter endure: to promote international peace, security and justice; to relieve and remove the blight of hunger, poverty and disease; and to protect the rights and liberties of every citizen.

The achievements of the United Nations are remarkable. When I was first here, there were just three United Nations operations overseas. Now over 120,000 men and women are deployed in twenty six missions across the world. You have helped to reduce conflict, you have offered humanitarian assistance to millions of people affected by natural disasters and other emergencies, and you have been deeply committed to tackling the effects of poverty in many parts of the world. But so much remains to be done…

New challenges have also emerged which have tested this organisation as much as its member states. One such is the struggle against terrorism. Another challenge is climate change, where careful account must be taken of the risks facing smaller, more vulnerable nations, many of them from the Commonwealth.

Queen Elizabeth addresses the General Assembly on July 6, at the United Nations in New York at the age of eighty-four. This was her first UN appearance since 1957, four years after being crowned.

It has perhaps always been the case that the waging of peace is the hardest form of leadership of all. I know of no single formula for success, but over the years I have observed that some attributes of leadership are universal, and are often about finding ways of encouraging people to combine their efforts, their talents, their insights, their enthusiasm and their inspiration, to work together.

Since I addressed you last, the Commonwealth, too, has grown vigorously to become a group of nations representing nearly two billion people. It gives its whole-hearted support to the significant contributions to the peace and stability of the world made by the United Nations and its Agencies. Last November, when I opened the Commonwealth Heads of Government Meeting in Trinidad and Tobago, I told the delegates that the Commonwealth had the opportunity to lead. Today I offer you the same message.

For over six decades the United Nations has helped to shape the international response to global dangers. The challenge now is to continue to show this clear and convening leadership while not losing sight of your ongoing work to secure the security, prosperity and dignity of our fellow human beings. When people in fifty-three years from now look back on us, they will doubtless view many of our practices as old-fashioned. But it is my hope that, when judged by future generations, our sincerity, our willingness to take a lead, and our determination to do the right thing, will stand the test of time.

In my lifetime, the United Nations has moved from being a high-minded aspiration to being a real force for common good. That of itself has been a signal achievement. But we are not gathered here to reminisce. In tomorrow's world, we must all work together as hard as ever if we are truly to be United Nations.

# 2010

*Speaking from The Chapel Royal at Hampton Court Palace, The Queen focussed on the 400th anniversary of the King James Bible, our success in the Paralympics and the importance of sport in bringing us all together.*

Over four hundred years ago, King James the Sixth of Scotland inherited the throne of England at a time when the Christian Church was deeply divided. Here at Hampton Court in 1604, he convened a conference of churchmen of all shades of opinion to discuss the future of Christianity in this country. The King agreed to commission a new translation of the Bible that was acceptable to all parties. This was to become the King James or Authorized Bible, which next year will be exactly four centuries old. Acknowledged as a masterpiece of English prose and the most vivid translation of the scriptures, the glorious language of this Bible has survived the turbulence of history and given many of us the most widely-recognised and beautiful descriptions of the birth of Jesus Christ which we celebrate today. The King James Bible was a major cooperative endeavour that required the efforts of dozens of the day's leading scholars. The whole enterprise was guided by an interest in reaching agreement for the wider benefit of the Christian Church, and to bring harmony to the Kingdoms of England and Scotland.

Four hundred years later, it is as important as ever to build communities and create harmony, and one of the most powerful ways of doing this is through sport and games. During this past year of abundant sporting events, I have seen for myself just how important sport is in bringing people together from all backgrounds, from all walks of life and from all age groups. In the parks of towns and cities, and on village greens up and down the country, countless thousands of people every week give up their time to participate in sport and exercise of all sorts, or simply encourage others to do so. These kinds of activity are common throughout the world and play a part in providing a different perspective on life.

Apart from developing physical fitness, sport and games can also teach vital social skills. None can be enjoyed without abiding by the rules, and no team can hope to succeed without cooperation between the players. This sort of positive team spirit can benefit communities, companies and enterprises of all kinds.

As the success of recent Paralympics bears witness, a love of sport also has the power to help rehabilitate. One only has to think of the injured men and women of the Armed Forces to see how an interest in games and sport can speed recovery and

renew a sense of purpose, enjoyment and comradeship. Right around the world, people gather to compete under standard rules and, in most cases, in a spirit of friendly rivalry. Competitors know that, to succeed, they must respect their opponents; very often, they like each other too.

Sportsmen and women often speak of the enormous pride they have in representing their country, a sense of belonging to a wider family. We see this vividly at the Commonwealth Games, for example, which is known to many as the Friendly Games and where I am sure you have noticed that it is always the competitors from the smallest countries who receive the loudest cheers.

People are capable of belonging to many communities, including a religious faith. King James may not have anticipated quite how important sport and games were to become in promoting harmony and common interests. But from the scriptures in the Bible which bears his name, we know that nothing is more satisfying than the feeling of belonging to a group who are dedicated to helping each other:

> *Therefore all things whatsoever ye would that men should to do to you,*
> *do ye even so to them.*

I wish you, and all those whom you love and care for, a very happy Christmas.

The Queen and Pope Benedict XVI meet school children outside the Palace of Holyroodhouse, The Queen's official residence in Scotland, during the Pope's four-day state visit to the UK.

# 2011

*TThis year saw many natural disasters. One a happier note, the first Black President of America, Barack Obama visited Britain, and in her Broadcast The Queen celebrated the marriage of Prince William to Kate Middleton.*

In this past year my family and I have been inspired by the courage and hope we have seen in so many ways in Britain, in the Commonwealth and around the world. We've seen that it's in hardship that we often find strength from our families; it's in adversity that new friendships are sometimes formed; and it's in a crisis that communities break down barriers and bind together to help one another.

Families, friends and communities often find a source of courage rising up from within. Indeed, sadly, it seems that it is tragedy that often draws out the most and the best from the human spirit. When Prince Philip and I visited Australia this year we saw for ourselves the effects of natural disaster in some of the areas devastated by floods, where in January so many people lost their lives and their livelihoods. We were moved by the way families and local communities held together to support each other.

Prince William travelled to New Zealand and Australia in the aftermath of earthquakes, cyclones and floods and saw how communities rose up to rescue the injured, comfort the bereaved and rebuild the cities and towns devastated by nature. The Prince of Wales also saw first hand the remarkable resilience of the human spirit after tragedy struck in a Welsh mining community, and how communities can work together to support their neighbours.

This past year has also seen some memorable and historic visits – to Ireland and from America. The spirit of friendship so evident in both these nations can fill us all with hope. Relationships that years ago were once so strained have through sorrow and forgiveness blossomed into long term friendship. It is through this lens of history that we should view the conflicts of today, and so give us hope for tomorrow.

Of course, family does not necessarily mean blood relatives but often a description of a community, organisation or nation. The Commonwealth is a family of fifty-three nations, all with a common bond, shared beliefs, mutual values and goals.

It is this which makes the Commonwealth a family of people in the truest sense, at ease with each other, enjoying its shared history and ready and willing to support its

On April 29 Prince William and Catherine Middleton were married at Westminster Cathedral, watched by millions around the world. In this official wedding photograph are: (from left) Prince Philip; The Prince of Wales; The Queen; Prince Harry; The Duke and Duchess of Cambridge; Catherine's father Michael; her mother Carole; her brother James and other bridesmaids and pageboys.

members in the direst of circumstances. They have always looked to the future, with a sense of camaraderie, warmth and mutual respect while still maintaining their individualism.

The importance of family has, of course, come home to Prince Philip and me personally this year with the marriages of two of our grandchildren, each in their own way a celebration of the God-given love that binds a family together.

For many this Christmas will not be easy. With our armed forces deployed around the world, thousands of service families face Christmas without their loved ones at home. The bereaved and the lonely will find it especially hard. And, as we all know, the world is going through difficult times. All this will affect our celebration of this great Christian festival. Finding hope in adversity is one of the themes of Christmas. Jesus was born into a world full of fear. The angels came to frightened shepherds with hope in their voices: 'Fear not', they urged, 'we bring you tidings of great joy, which shall be to all people. For unto you is born this day in the City of David a Saviour who is Christ the Lord.'

Although we are capable of great acts of kindness, history teaches us that we sometimes need saving from ourselves – from our recklessness or our greed. God sent into the world a unique person – neither a philosopher nor a general (important though they are) – but a Saviour, with the power to forgive. Forgiveness lies at the heart of the Christian faith. It can heal broken families, it can restore friendships and it can reconcile divided communities. It is in forgiveness that we feel the power of God's love.

In the last verse of this beautiful carol, 'O Little Town of Bethlehem', there's a prayer:

> *O Holy Child of Bethlehem*
> *Descend to us we pray*
> *Cast out our sin*
> *And enter in*
> *Be born in us today.*

It is my prayer that on this Christmas day we might all find room in our lives for the message of the angels and for the love of God through Christ our Lord. I wish you all a very happy Christmas.

President Obama and his wife Michelle paid a two-day state visit to London in May 2011. Here The Queen and President Obama pose before a state banquet at Buckingham Palace.

# 2012 ~ 2021

## *The* DIAMOND YEARS

The Queen records her Christmas message to the UK and
Commonwealth in 3D for the first time in 2012, in the White
Drawing Room at Buckingham Palace.

On 9 September 2015, at eighty-nine years and 141 days old, The Queen became Great Britain's longest-ever reigning monarch, surpassing Queen Victoria, her great-great grandmother. On 13 October 2016, she became the *world's* longest reigning monarch. Notwithstanding, The Queen also celebrated sixty and sixty-five years as monarch in 2012 and 2017. On 20 November 2017, she had been married to Prince Philip for seventy years.

The London Olympic and Paralympic Games in 2012 did not disappoint, nor did our sportsmen and women, winning twenty-nine golds, seventeen silvers and nineteen bronzes, to place Great Britain third in the international medals table. In the Paralympics we were also placed third.

The Arab Spring of early 2010 led to uprisings, protests, riots and fighting in Tunisia, Algeria, Libya, Egypt, Syria, Bahrain and Yemen. On 29 August 2013, Prime Minister Cameron lost the parliamentary vote for military action in Syria by thirteen votes. Syria's civil war dragged on and on, continuing to this day. At the time of writing, more than 500,000 people have been killed or are missing.

The emergence of ISIL, now better known as ISIS, married Muslim fundamentalism with terrorism. This ideology proved a heady cocktail to many. Frequent terrorist attacks took place across Europe, largely from dissident supporters of ISIS or lone wolves claiming allegiance to the group, which killed hundreds of innocent people whilst injuring many more. Eventually, with American-led forces, Iraq was liberated and ISIS was forced back to Syria. But it is still active.

During this decade, four young women had a profound impact on us all. On 9 October 2012, fifteen-year-old Pakistani schoolgirl Malala Yousafzai was shot and nearly killed by a Tehrik-i-Taliban Pakistani operator while on a bus on her way to school. For her writings, activism, bravery and courage Malala was awarded the Nobel Peace Prize in 2014, the youngest ever recipient. She

eventually settled in England, where she graduated from Oxford University in 2020 and continues to fight for the right for education and equality for girls through her Malala Fund.

In August 2018, rather than go to school, Swedish student Greta Thunberg started a strike for climate change mitigation outside the Swedish Parliament. The actions of this determined fifteen-year-old caught the world's imagination and started a grown-up conversation amongst global leaders about the dangers of climate change. She won the *Prix Liberté* and was nominated three times for the Nobel Peace Prize.

On 20 January 2021, aged twenty-two, a previously little-known Black American student, Amanda Gorman, recited her poem 'The Hill We Climb' at President Biden's inauguration and spoke a message of truth and hope to millions, becoming the absolute star of the ceremony.

In September 2021, Emma Raducanu surprised the sporting world when she won the US Open tennis championships aged just 18. She never dropped a set. Virginia Wade (who was in the crowd watching) was the last British player to win the tournament back in 1968. Emma was crowned BBC's Sports Personality of the Year in December, 2021 and then awarded an MBE.

A number of issues bumped into one another: The result of the Brexit referendum in 2016 was close (52% for, 48% against) and led to Prime Minister Cameron resigning. The concept of averting climate change still had no real ownership amongst global leaders, as the UN Climate Change Conference (COP 26), hosted in Glasgow in November 2021, illustrated. There were two catastrophic fires, one at Grenfell Tower in north London that killed seventy-two people and another at Notre Dame de Paris, where the cathedral roof caught fire.

Black female activists Alicia Garza, Patrisse Cullors, and Opal Tometi created the #BlackLivesMatter project in response to the acquittal of Trayvon Martin's murderer, George Zimmerman. The organisation is now a member-led global network of more than forty chapters. 'Taking the knee', a symbolic gesture against racism, started when Colin Kaepernick, an NFL player, dropped to his knee on 1 September 2016. The killing of George Floyd in May 2020 by Derek Chauvin, a police officer in Minneapolis, caused widespread global protests and led to sportsmen and women across the world 'taking the knee' in solidarity.

It was the changing of the presidential guards in America when Republican President Trump's dysfunctional four-year reign came to an end in 2021, following his loss to Democrat candidate Joe Biden. The world watched in disbelief at the attempted coup on Capitol Hill on 6 January 2021. In the UK, Prime Minister Johnson succeeded Prime Minister May on 23 July 2019, after she resigned following lack of Parliamentary support for her Brexit plans.

The Me Too movement (#MeToo) was initially created in 2006 by activist Tarana Burke but came to the fore again in 2017 following the allegations of a dozen women accusing Harvey Weinstein, a prominent Hollywood film producer, of sexually harassing, assaulting or raping them. He was sentenced to twenty-three years in jail. Me Too organisations have been created in thirty-three other countries.

Same-sex marriages finally became law in England and Wales in July 2013, in Scotland in February 2014 and in Northern Ireland in January 2020.

The Covid-19 pandemic started some time in December 2019, with the first case identified in the central Chinese city of Wuhan. Wuhan itself, a city of 11 million, was locked down on 23 January 2020. The first case in the UK was confirmed on 29 January 2020. Britain was locked down twice in 2020 and once in 2021 to limit spread of the highly contagious virus and scientists worldwide focused their attention on creating an effective vaccine. Professor Sarah Gilbert, a British vaccinologist, and her team at Oxford University, in collaboration with pharmaceutical manufacturer AstraZeneca plc, produced a working vaccine on 23 November 2020 and vaccinations started being administered in the UK on 8 December 2020.

In other news, Prince Harry married American actress Meghan Markle on 19 May 2018, garnering an estimated global audience of 1.9 billion. In 2020, they formally stepped back from their roles as members of the royal family, emigrating to the US. We said goodbye to many significant people during this decade including Neil Armstrong (2012) Nelson Mandela and Baroness Thatcher (2013), writer Maya Angelou and actor Lauren Bacall (2014), Muhammed Ali (2019) and author and Nobel laureate Toni Morrison. We also lost a slew of magnificent musicians, among them BB King (2015), Prince, David Bowie and Leonard Cohen (2016) and Aretha Franklin (2018).

Finally, and most pertinently to the subject of this book, we lost the man The Queen called her 'strength and stay', HRH Prince Philip, The Duke of Edinburgh, on 9 April 2021.

# 5 JUNE 2012
# THE DIAMOND JUBILEE,

*In 2012 The Queen became only the second British monarch in history to celebrate sixty years on the throne. The whole country became involved in celebrating her reign. Thousands of events took place around the country and The Queen made this short address to thank everyone.*

The events that I have attended to mark my Diamond Jubilee have been a humbling experience. It has touched me deeply to see so many thousands of families, neighbours and friends celebrating together in such a happy atmosphere.

But Prince Philip and I want to take this opportunity to offer our special thanks and appreciation to all those who have had a hand in organising these Jubilee celebrations. It has been a massive challenge, and I am sure that everyone who has enjoyed these festive occasions realises how much work has been involved.

I hope that memories of all this year's happy events will brighten our lives for many years to come. I will continue to treasure and draw inspiration from the countless kindnesses shown to me in this country and throughout the Commonwealth

Thank you all.

*Opposite above*: The Queen sits between the Duchess and the Duke of Cambridge as they enjoy a display at Vernon Park, Nottingham, as part of a Diamond Jubilee visit to the area. *Below:* Over 1000 small boats braved the unseasonable rain and sailed up the River Thames in London as part of the Diamond Jubilee celebrations on 3 June, 2012. Here, they pass the Houses of Parliament.

# 2012

*This was an eventful year. The Queen reached her Diamond Jubilee, and appeared alongside James Bond in a celebratory video! London hosted the Olympic and Paralympic Games, and in her Christmas Broadcast The Queen praised the skill and dedication of the athletes.*

This past year has been one of great celebration for many. The enthusiasm which greeted the Diamond Jubilee was, of course, especially memorable for me and my family. It was humbling that so many chose to mark the anniversary of a duty which passed to me sixty years ago. People of all ages took the trouble to take part in various ways and in many nations. But perhaps most striking of all was to witness the strength of fellowship and friendship among those who had gathered together on these occasions.

Prince Philip and I were joined by our family on the River Thames as we paid tribute to those who have shaped the United Kingdom's past and future as a maritime nation, and welcomed a wonderful array of craft, large and small, from across the Commonwealth. On the barges and the bridges and the banks of the river there were people who had taken their places to cheer through the mist, undaunted by the rain. That day there was a tremendous sense of common determination to celebrate, triumphing over the elements.

That same spirit was also in evidence from the moment the Olympic flame arrived on these shores. The flame itself drew hundreds and thousands of people on its journey around the British Isles, and was carried by every kind of deserving individual, many nominated for their own extraordinary service.

As London hosted a splendid summer of sport, all those who saw the achievement and courage at the Olympic and Paralympic Games were further inspired by the skill, dedication, training and teamwork of our athletes. In pursuing their own sporting goals, they gave the rest of us the opportunity to share something of the excitement and drama.

We were reminded, too, that the success of these great festivals depended to an enormous degree upon the dedication and effort of an army of volunteers. Those public-spirited people came forward in the great tradition of all those who devote themselves to keeping others safe, supported and comforted.

At the instigation of her grandsons, Princes William and Harry, The Queen took part in a spoof video, also starring James Bond actor Daniel Craig, which was shown as part of the Olympic opening ceremony.

The Queen is all smiles during a Diamond Jubilee walkabout at the Glades shopping centre in Bromley, south London.

For many, Christmas is also a time for coming together. But for others, service will come first. Those serving in our Armed Forces, in our Emergency Services and in our hospitals, whose sense of duty takes them away from family and friends, will be missing those they love. And those who have lost loved ones may find this day especially full of memories. That's why it's important at this time of year to reach out beyond our familiar relationships to think of those who are on their own.

At Christmas I am always struck by how the spirit of togetherness lies also at the heart of the Christmas story. A young mother and a dutiful father with their baby were joined by poor shepherds and visitors from afar. They came with their gifts to worship the Christ child. From that day on He has inspired people to commit themselves to the best interests of others.

This is the time of year when we remember that God sent his only son 'to serve, not to be served'. He restored love and service to the centre of our lives in the person of Jesus Christ. It is my prayer this Christmas Day that his example and teaching will continue to bring people together to give the best of themselves in the service of others.

The carol, 'In the Bleak Midwinter', ends by asking a question of all of us who know the Christmas story, of how God gave himself to us in humble service: 'What can I give him, poor as I am? If I were a shepherd, I would bring a lamb; if I were a wise man, I would do my part'. The carol gives the answer, 'Yet what I can I give him – give my heart'. I wish you all a very happy Christmas.

# 2013

*In a year blighted by the continuing civil war in Syria, The Queen chose the theme of reflection for her Christmas Broadcast. She also looked forward to the Commonwealth Games. A personal moment of happiness was the arrival of a great-grandchild, Prince George Alexander Louis Cambridge.*

I once knew someone who spent a year in a plaster cast recovering from an operation on his back. He read a lot, and thought a lot, and felt miserable. Later, he realised this time of forced retreat from the world had helped him to understand the world more clearly.

We all need to get the balance right between action and reflection. With so many distractions, it is easy to forget to pause and take stock. Be it through contemplation, prayer, or even keeping a diary, many have found the practice of quiet personal reflection surprisingly rewarding, even discovering greater spiritual depth to their lives. Reflection can take many forms. When families and friends come together at Christmas, it's often a time for happy memories and reminiscing. Our thoughts are with those we have loved who are no longer with us. We also remember those who through doing their duty cannot be at home for Christmas, such as workers in essential or emergency services.

And especially at this time of year we think of the men and women serving overseas in our armed forces. We are forever grateful to all those who put themselves at risk to keep us safe. Service and duty are not just the guiding principles of yesteryear; they have an enduring value which spans the generations.

I myself had cause to reflect this year, at Westminster Abbey, on my own pledge of service made in that great church on Coronation Day sixty years earlier. The anniversary reminded me of the remarkable changes that have occurred since the Coronation, many of them for the better; and of the things that have remained constant, such as the importance of family, friendship and good neighbourliness.

But reflection is not just about looking back. I and many others are looking forward to the Commonwealth Games in Glasgow next year. The baton relay left London in October and is now the other side of the world, on its way across seventy nations and territories before arriving in Scotland next summer. Its journey is a reminder that the Commonwealth can offer us a fresh view of life.

*Here at home my own family is a little larger this Christmas. As so many of you will know, the arrival of a baby gives everyone the chance to contemplate the future with renewed happiness and hope.*

My son Charles summed this up at the recent meeting in Sri Lanka. He spoke of the Commonwealth's 'family ties' that are a source of encouragement to many. Like any family there can be differences of opinion. But however strongly they're expressed they are held within the common bond of friendship and shared experiences.

Here at home my own family is a little larger this Christmas. As so many of you will know, the arrival of a baby gives everyone the chance to contemplate the future with renewed happiness and hope. For the new parents, life will never be quite the same again! As with all who are christened, George was baptised into a joyful faith of Christian duty and service. After the christening, we gathered for the traditional photograph. It was a happy occasion, bringing together four generations.

In the year ahead, I hope you will have time to pause for moments of quiet reflection. As the man in the plaster cast discovered, the results can sometimes be surprising. For Christians, as for all people of faith, reflection, meditation and prayer help us to renew ourselves in God's love, as we strive daily to become better people. The Christmas message shows us that this love is for everyone. There is no one beyond its reach.

On the first Christmas, in the fields above Bethlehem, as they sat in the cold of night watching their resting sheep, the local shepherds must have had no shortage of time for reflection. Suddenly all this was to change. These humble shepherds were the first to hear and ponder the wondrous news of the birth of Christ – the first noel – the joy of which we celebrate today. I wish you all a very happy Christmas.

The Duke and Duchess of Cambridge with their son, christened George Alexander Louis Cambridge by the Archbishop of Canterbury on October 23, 2013.

# 2014

*This year, themes of reconciliation and remembrance were very much in The Queen's mind when she recorded her Broadcast. In November she attended a ceremony held at the Tower of London, where an astonishing art installation covered the Moat in ceramic poppies.*

In the ruins of the old Coventry Cathedral is a sculpture of a man and a woman reaching out to embrace each other. The sculptor was inspired by the story of a woman who crossed Europe on foot after the war to find her husband. Casts of the same sculpture can be found in Belfast and Berlin, and it is simply called 'Reconciliation'.

Reconciliation is the peaceful end to conflict, and we were reminded of this in August when countries on both sides of the First World War came together to remember in peace. The ceramic poppies at the Tower of London drew millions, and the only possible reaction to seeing them and walking among them was silence. For every poppy a life; and a reminder of the grief of loved ones left behind. No-one who fought in that war is still alive, but we remember their sacrifice and indeed the sacrifice of all those in the armed forces who serve and protect us today. In 1914, many people thought the war would be over by Christmas, but sadly by then the trenches were dug and the future shape of the war in Europe was set. But, as we know, something remarkable did happen that Christmas, exactly a hundred years ago today. Without any instruction or command, the shooting stopped and German and British soldiers met in No Man's Land. Photographs were taken and gifts exchanged. It was a Christmas truce.

Truces are not a new idea. In the ancient world a truce was declared for the duration of the Olympic Games and wars and battles were put on hold. Sport has a wonderful way of bringing together people and nations, as we saw this year in Glasgow when over seventy countries took part in the Commonwealth Games. It is no accident that they are known as the Friendly Games. As well as promoting dialogue between nations, the Commonwealth Games pioneered the inclusion of para-sports within each day's events. As with the Invictus Games that followed, the courage, determination and talent of the athletes captured our imagination as well as breaking down divisions.

The benefits of reconciliation were clear to see when I visited Belfast in June. While my tour of the set of *Game of Thrones* may have gained most attention, my visit to the Crumlin Road Gaol will remain vividly in my mind. What was once a prison during the troubles is now a place of hope and fresh purpose; a reminder of what is possible when

people reach out to one another, rather like the couple in the sculpture. Of course, reconciliation takes different forms. In Scotland after the referendum many felt great disappointment, while others felt great relief; and bridging these differences will take time. Bringing reconciliation to war or emergency zones is an even harder task, and I have been deeply touched this year by the selflessness of aid workers and medical volunteers who have gone abroad to help victims of conflict or of diseases like Ebola, often at great personal risk.

For me, the life of Jesus Christ, the Prince of Peace, whose birth we celebrate today, is an inspiration and an anchor in my life. A role-model of reconciliation and forgiveness, he stretched out his hands in love, acceptance and healing. Christ's example has taught me to seek to respect and value all people of whatever faith or none.

Sometimes it seems that reconciliation stands little chance in the face of war and discord. But, as the Christmas truce a century ago reminds us, peace and goodwill have lasting power in the hearts of men and women.

On that chilly Christmas Eve in 1914 many of the German forces sang 'Silent Night', its haunting melody inching across the line. That carol is still much-loved today, a legacy of the Christmas truce, and a reminder to us all that even in the unlikeliest of places hope can still be found. A very happy Christmas to you all.

The Queen and Prince Philip walk among 'Blood Swept Lands and Seas of Red' – a commemorative art installation at the Tower of London to mark the centenary of the outbreak of World War One. In November, the Moat at the Tower was filled with 888,246 ceramic poppies created by artist Paul Cummins; each representing a fallen British or Commonwealth soldier.

# 2015

*The tradition of the Christmas tree, casting its lights of hope and inspiration, was the leading theme of The Queen's Broadcast this year, although among the moments of darkness to which she alludes were the terrorist attacks in Paris and Tunisia that killed hundreds of people.*

At this time of year, few sights evoke more feelings of cheer and goodwill than the twinkling lights of a Christmas tree. The popularity of a tree at Christmas is due in part to my great-great grandparents, Queen Victoria and Prince Albert. After this touching picture was published, many families wanted a Christmas tree of their own, and the custom soon spread.

In 1949, I spent Christmas in Malta as a newly-married naval wife. We have returned to that island over the years, including last month for a meeting of Commonwealth leaders; and this year I met another group of leaders: The Queen's Young Leaders, an inspirational group, each of them a symbol of hope in their own Commonwealth communities.

Gathering round the tree gives us a chance to think about the year ahead – I am looking forward to a busy 2016, though I have been warned I may have Happy Birthday sung to me more than once or twice. It also allows us to reflect on the year that has passed, as we think of those who are far away or no longer with us. Many people say the first Christmas after losing a loved one is particularly hard. But it's also a time to remember all that we have to be thankful for.

It is true that the world has had to confront moments of darkness this year, but the Gospel of John contains a verse of great hope, often read at Christmas carol services: 'The light shines in the darkness, and the darkness has not overcome it.'

One cause for thankfulness this summer was marking seventy years since the end of the Second World War. On VJ Day, we honoured the remaining veterans of that terrible conflict in the Far East, as well as remembering the thousands who never returned. The procession from Horse Guards Parade to Westminster Abbey must have been one of the slowest ever, because so many people wanted to say 'thank you' to them.

At the end of that War, the people of Oslo began sending an annual gift of a Christmas tree for Trafalgar Square. It has five hundred lightbulbs and is enjoyed not just by Christians but by people of all faiths, and of none. At the very top sits a bright star, to represent the Star of Bethlehem.

The custom of topping a tree also goes back to Prince Albert's time. For his family's tree, he chose an angel, helping to remind us that the focus of the Christmas story is on one particular family. For Joseph and Mary, the circumstances of Jesus's birth – in a stable – were far from ideal, but worse was to come as the family was forced to flee the country. It's no surprise that such a human story still captures our imagination and continues to inspire all of us who are Christians, the world over.

Despite being displaced and persecuted throughout his short life, Christ's unchanging message was not one of revenge or violence but simply that we should love one another. Although it is not an easy message to follow, we shouldn't be discouraged; rather, it inspires us to try harder: to be thankful for the people who bring love and happiness into our own lives, and to look for ways of spreading that love to others, whenever and wherever we can.

*One of the joys of living a long life is watching one's children, then grandchildren, then great grandchildren, help decorate the Christmas tree*

One of the joys of living a long life is watching one's children, then grandchildren, then great-grandchildren, help decorate the Christmas tree. And this year my family has a new member to join in the fun!

The customary decorations have changed little in the years since that picture of Victoria and Albert's tree first appeared, although of course electric lights have replaced the candles. There's an old saying that 'it is better to light a candle than curse the darkness'. There are millions of people lighting candles of hope in our world today. Christmas is a good time to be thankful for them, and for all that brings light to our lives. I wish you a very happy Christmas.

# 2016

*In the year of her ninetieth birthday, The Queen dwelt on the theme of inspiration in her Broadcast. There was plenty available: she congratulated Team GB on their splendid Olympic performance and paid tribute to the dedication of thousands of volunteers and supporters of the 600 charities of which she was then patron.*

There was a time when British Olympic medal winners became household names because there were so few of them. But the 67 medals at this year's Games in Rio and 147 at the Paralympics meant that the GB medallists' reception at Buckingham Palace was a crowded and happy event. Throughout the Commonwealth there were equally joyful celebrations. Grenada, the Bahamas, Jamaica and New Zealand won more medals per head of population than any other countries. Many of this year's winners spoke of being inspired by athletes of previous generations. Inspiration fed their aspiration; and having discovered abilities they scarcely knew they had, these athletes are now inspiring others.

*To be inspirational you don't have to save lives or win medals. I often draw strength from meeting ordinary people doing extraordinary things*

A few months ago, I saw inspiration of a different kind when I opened the new Cambridge base of the East Anglian Air Ambulance, where Prince William works as a helicopter pilot. It was not hard to be moved by the dedication of the highly skilled doctors, paramedics and crew, who are called out on average five times a day.

But to be inspirational you don't have to save lives or win medals. I often draw strength from meeting ordinary people doing extraordinary things: volunteers, carers, community organisers and good neighbours; unsung heroes whose quiet dedication makes them special.

They are an inspiration to those who know them, and their lives frequently embody a truth expressed by Mother Teresa, from this year Saint Teresa of Calcutta. She once said, 'Not all of us can do great things. But we can do small things with great love.'

The Queen and Duke of Edinburgh wave to guests attending The Patrons' Lunch, part of a weekend of celebrations for the monarch's ninetieth birthday. Over 10,000 people were invited from over 600 charities and organisations of which The Queen was then Patron.

This has been the experience of two remarkable organisations, The Duke of Edinburgh's Award and the Prince's Trust, which are sixty and forty years old this year. These started as small initiatives but have grown beyond any expectations, and continue to transform young people's lives.

To mark my 90th birthday, volunteers and supporters of the six hundred charities of which I have been patron came to a lunch in The Mall. Many of these organisations are modest in size but inspire me with the work they do. From giving friendship and support to our veterans, the elderly or the bereaved; to championing music and dance; providing animal welfare; or protecting our fields and forests, their selfless devotion and generosity of spirit is an example to us all.

The Queen and Prince Phillip bid farewell to Columbia's President Juan Manuel Santos and his wife Maria Clemencia de Santos following their state visit in November 2016.

When people face a challenge they sometimes talk about taking a deep breath to find courage or strength. In fact, the word 'inspire' literally means 'to breathe in'. But even with the inspiration of others, it's understandable that we sometimes think the world's problems are so big that we can do little to help. On our own, we cannot end wars or wipe out injustice, but the cumulative impact of thousands of small acts of goodness can be bigger than we imagine.

At Christmas, our attention is drawn to the birth of a baby some two thousand years ago. It was the humblest of beginnings, and his parents, Joseph and Mary, did not think they were important. Jesus Christ lived obscurely for most of his life, and never travelled far. He was maligned and rejected by many, though he had done no wrong. And yet, billions of people now follow his teaching and find in him the guiding light for their lives. I am one of them because Christ's example helps me see the value of doing small things with great love, whoever does them and whatever they themselves believe.

The message of Christmas reminds us that inspiration is a gift to be given as well as received, and that love begins small but always grows I wish you all a very happy

Christmas.

# 2017

*As the Queen acknowledged in her Broadcast, this year was in many ways overshadowed by dreadful events: including the Manchester Arena Bombings and the Grenfell Tower fire. There was cause for joy too, as she and Prince Philip celebrated seventy years of marriage.*

Sixty years ago today, I spoke about the speed of technological change, in what was my first televised Christmas broadcast. At the time, it felt like a landmark: 'Television has made it possible for many of you to see me in your homes on Christmas Day. My own family often gather round to watch television as they are at this moment, and that is how I imagine you now.'

Six decades on, the presenter of that broadcast has 'evolved' somewhat, as has the technology she described. Back then, who could have imagined that people would one day be following this Christmas message on laptops and mobile phones? But I'm also struck by something that hasn't changed. That, whatever the technology, many of you will be watching or listening to this at home.

We think of our homes as places of warmth, familiarity and love; of shared stories and memories, which is perhaps why at this time of year so many return to where they grew up. There is a timeless simplicity to the pull of home. For many, the idea of 'home' reaches beyond a physical building – to a home, town or city. This Christmas, I think of London and Manchester, whose powerful identities shone through over the past twelve months in the face of appalling attacks. In Manchester, those targeted included children who had gone to see their favourite singer. A few days after the bombing, I had the privilege of meeting some of the young survivors and their parents. I describe that hospital visit as a 'privilege' because the patients I met were an example to us all, showing extraordinary bravery and resilience. Indeed, many of those who survived the attack came together just days later for a benefit concert. It was a powerful reclaiming of the ground, and of the city those young people call home.

We expect our homes to be a place of safety – 'sanctuary' even – which makes it all the more shocking when the comfort they provide is shattered. A few weeks ago, The Prince of Wales visited the Caribbean in the aftermath of hurricanes that destroyed entire communities.  And here in London, who can forget the sheer awfulness of the Grenfell Tower fire?

The Queen reviews The King's Troop, Royal Horse Artillery at Hyde
Park on their seventieth anniversary in October.  This is a
ceremonial unit of the British Army. All its soldiers are trained to
drive teams of six horses, pulling each of six First World War
pounder guns to fire salutes on state occasions.

Our thoughts and prayers are with all those who died and those who lost so much; and we are indebted to members of the emergency services who risked their own lives, this past year, saving others. Many of them, of course, will not be at home today because they are working, to protect us.

Reflecting on these events makes me grateful for the blessings of home and family, and in particular for seventy years of marriage. I don't know that anyone had invented the term 'platinum' for a seventieth wedding anniversary when I was born. You weren't expected to be around that long. Even Prince Philip has decided it's time to slow down a little – having, as he economically put it, 'done his bit'. But I know his support and unique sense of humour will remain as strong as ever, as we enjoy spending time this Christmas with our family and look forward to welcoming new members into it next year.

*We think of our homes as places of warmth, familiarity and love, of shared stories and memories, which is perhaps at this time of year so many return to where they grew up.*

In 2018 I will open my home to a different type of family: the leaders of the fifty-two nations of the Commonwealth, as they gather in the UK for a summit. The Commonwealth has an inspiring way of bringing people together, be it through the Commonwealth Games – which begins in a few months' time on Australia's Gold Coast – or through bodies like the Commonwealth Youth Orchestra and Choir: a reminder of how truly vibrant this international family is.

Today we celebrate Christmas, which itself is sometimes described as a festival of the home. Families travel long distances to be together. Volunteers and charities, as well as many churches, arrange meals for the homeless and those who would otherwise be alone on Christmas Day. We remember the birth of Jesus Christ whose only sanctuary was a stable in Bethlehem. He knew rejection, hardship and persecution; and yet it is Jesus Christ's generous love and example that has inspired me through good times and bad.

Whatever your own experiences this year; wherever and however you are watching or listening, I wish you a peaceful and very happy Christmas.

# 2018

*In this year's Broadcast, The Queen reflected on what had been personally a happy year for her family, with highlights including the birth of the Duke and Duchess of Cambridge's third child, Louis, in April, and the wedding of Prince Harry to Meghan Markle at St George's Chapel, Windsor in the May sunshine.*

For many, the service of Nine Lessons and Carols from King's College, Cambridge, is when Christmas begins. Listened to by millions of people around the world, it starts with a chorister singing the first verse of 'Once in Royal David's City'.

The priest who introduced this service to King's College chapel, exactly one hundred years ago, was Eric Milner-White. He had served as a military chaplain in the First World War. Just six weeks after the Armistice, he wanted a new kind of service which – with its message of peace and goodwill – spoke to the needs of the times.

2018 has been a year of centenaries. The Royal Air Force celebrated its hundreth anniversary with a memorable fly-past demonstrating a thrilling unity of purpose and execution. We owe them and all our Armed Services our deepest gratitude.

My father served in the Royal Navy during the First World War. He was a midshipman in HMS *Collingwood* at the Battle of Jutland in 1916. The British fleet lost fourteen ships and 6,000 men in that engagement. My father wrote in a letter: 'How and why we were not hit beats me'. Like others, he lost friends in the war. At Christmas, we become keenly aware of loved ones who have died, whatever the circumstances. But of course, we would not grieve if we did not love.

Closer to home, it's been a busy year for my family, with two weddings and two babies – and another child expected soon. It helps to keep a grandmother well occupied. We have had other celebrations too, including the seventieth birthday of The Prince of Wales.

Some cultures believe a long life brings wisdom. I'd like to think so. Perhaps part of that wisdom is to recognise some of life's baffling paradoxes, such as the way human beings have a huge propensity for good, and yet a capacity for evil. Even the power of faith, which frequently inspires great generosity and self-sacrifice, can fall victim to tribalism. But through the many changes I have seen over the years, faith, family and friendship have been not only a constant for me but a source of personal comfort and reassurance.

In April, the Commonwealth Heads of Government met in London. My father welcomed just eight countries to the first such meeting in 1948. Now the Commonwealth includes fifty-three countries with 2.4 billion people, a third of the world's population. Its strength lies in the bonds of affection it promotes, and a common desire to live in a better, more peaceful world. Even with the most deeply held differences, treating the other person with respect and as a fellow human being is always a good first step towards greater understanding. Indeed, the Commonwealth Games, held this year on Australia's Gold Coast, are known universally as the 'Friendly Games' because of their emphasis on goodwill and mutual respect.

The Christmas story retains its appeal since it doesn't provide theoretical explanations for the puzzles of life. Instead it's about the birth of a child and the hope that birth – 2,000 years ago – brought to the world. Only a few people acknowledged Jesus when he was born. Now billions follow him. I believe his message of peace-on-earth and goodwill-to-all is never out of date. It can be heeded by everyone. It's needed as much as ever. A very happy Christmas to you all.

The newly-married Duke and Duchess of Sussex - Prince Harry and American actor Meghan Markle - leave St George's Chapel, Windsor en route for a lunchtime reception at Windsor Castle, before an evening party hosted by Prince Charles at Frogmore House, Windsor.

# 2019

*This year saw the seventy-fifth anniversary of the D-Day landings. In her Broadcast*
*The Queen reflected on the spirit of reconciliation, and the work of many people since*
*the War to mend differences. She also recalled being as transfixed as the rest of us*
*while watching the moon landings, fifty years ago.*

As a child, I never imagined that one day a man would walk on the moon. Yet this year we marked the fiftieth anniversary of the famous Apollo 11 mission. As those historic pictures were beamed backed to earth, millions of us sat transfixed to our television screens, as we watched Neil Armstrong taking a small step for man and a giant leap for mankind and, indeed, for womankind. It's a reminder for us all that giant leaps often start with small steps.

This year we marked another important anniversary: D-Day. On 6 June 1944, some one hundred and fifty-six thousand British, Canadian and American forces landed in Northern France. It was the largest ever seaborne invasion and was delayed due to bad weather. I well remember the look of concern on my father's face. He knew the secret D-Day plans but could of course share that burden with no-one.

For the seventy-fifth anniversary of that decisive battle, in a true spirit of reconciliation, those who had formerly been sworn enemies came together in friendly commemorations either side of the Channel, putting past differences behind them. Such reconciliation seldom happens overnight. It takes patience and time to rebuild trust, and progress often comes through small steps. Since the end of the Second World War, many charities, groups and organisations have worked to promote peace and unity around the world, bringing together those who have been on opposing sides. By being willing to put past differences behind us and move forward together, we honour the freedom and democracy once won for us at so great a cost.

The challenges many people face today may be different to those once faced by my generation, but I have been struck by how new generations have brought a similar sense of purpose to issues such as protecting our environment and our climate.My family and I are also inspired by the men and women of our emergency services and Armed Forces; and at Christmas we remember all those on duty at home and abroad, who are helping those in need and keeping us and our families safe and secure.

With photographs of her exapnded family nearby, The Queen records her 2019 Christmas Broadcast from Windsor Castle.

Two hundred years on from the birth of my great, great grandmother, Queen Victoria, Prince Philip and I have been delighted to welcome our eighth great grandchild into our family. Of course, at the heart of the Christmas story lies the birth of a child: a seemingly small and insignificant step overlooked by many in Bethlehem. But in time, through his teaching and by his example, Jesus Christ would show the world how small steps taken in faith and in hope can overcome long-held differences and deep-seated divisions to bring harmony and understanding. Many of us already try to follow in his footsteps. The path, of course, is not always smooth, and may at times this year have felt quite bumpy, but small steps can make a world of difference. As Christmas dawned, church congregations around the world joined in singing 'It Came Upon the Midnight Clear'. Like many timeless carols, it speaks not just of the coming of Jesus Christ into a divided world, many years ago, but also of the relevance, even today, of the angels' message of peace and goodwill.

It's a timely reminder of what positive things can be achieved when people set aside past differences and come together in the spirit of friendship and reconciliation. And, as we all look forward to the start of a new decade, it's worth remembering that it is often the small steps, not the giant leaps, that bring about the most lasting change. And so, I wish you all a very happy Christmas.

# 2020

*As might be expected, the devastating effects of the pandemic dominated The Queen's Broadcast for 2020. She praised the many people who had risen to the challenge of such a difficult and tragic year, volunteering in their communities, or working in hospitals and in the emergency services.*

Every year we herald the coming of Christmas by turning on the lights. And light does more than create a festive mood – light brings hope. For Christians, Jesus is 'the light of the world', but we can't celebrate his birth today in quite the usual way. People of all faiths have been unable to gather as they would wish for their festivals, such as Passover, Easter, Eid, and Vaisakhi. But we need life to go on. Last month, fireworks lit up the sky around Windsor, as Hindus, Sikhs and Jains celebrated Diwali, the festival of lights, providing joyous moments of hope and unity – despite social distancing.

Remarkably, a year that has necessarily kept people apart has, in many ways, brought us closer. Across the Commonwealth, my family and I have been inspired by stories of people volunteering in their communities, helping those in need. In the United Kingdom and around the world, people have risen magnificently to the challenges of the year, and I am so proud and moved by this quiet, indomitable spirit. To our young people in particular I say thank you for the part you have played.

This year, we celebrated International Nurses' Day, on the 200th anniversary of the birth of Florence Nightingale. As with other nursing pioneers like Mary Seacole, Florence Nightingale shone a lamp of hope across the world. Today, our front-line services still shine that lamp for us — supported by the amazing achievements of modern science – and we owe them a debt of gratitude. We continue to be inspired by the kindness of strangers and draw comfort that – even on the darkest nights – there is hope in the new dawn.

Jesus touched on this with the parable of the Good Samaritan. The man who is robbed and left at the roadside is saved by someone who did not share his religion or culture. This wonderful story of kindness is still as relevant today. Good Samaritans have emerged across society showing care and respect for all, regardless of gender, race or background, reminding us that each one of us is special and equal in the eyes of God. The teachings of Christ have served as my inner light, as has the sense of purpose we can find in coming together to worship.

In November, we commemorated another hero – though nobody knows his name. The Tomb of the Unknown Warrior isn't a large memorial, but everyone entering Westminster Abbey has to walk around his resting place, honouring this unnamed combatant of the First World War — a symbol of selfless duty and ultimate sacrifice. The Unknown Warrior was not exceptional. That's the point. He represents millions like him who throughout our history have put the lives of others above their own, and will be doing so today. For me, this is a source of enduring hope in difficult and unpredictable times.

Of course, for many, this time of year will be tinged with sadness: some mourning the loss of those dear to them, and others missing friends and family-members distanced for safety, when all they'd really want for Christmas is a simple hug or a squeeze of the hand. If you are among them, you are not alone, and let me assure you of my thoughts and prayers.

The Bible tells how a star appeared in the sky, its light guiding the shepherds and wise men to the scene of Jesus's birth. Let the light of Christmas  – the spirit of selflessness, love and above all hope  – guide us in the times ahead. It is in that spirit that I wish you a very happy Christmas.

The Duke and Duchess of Cambridge, The Queen, Prince Charles and Camilla, Duchess of Cornwall attend an event in December at Windsor Castle to thank all local volunteers and key workers in the Berkshire area for their efforts over Christmas.

# 1ST NOVEMBER 2021
# ADDRESS TO THE COP26

*On her doctors' advice, The Queen decided not to attend the Conference of the Parties in Glasgow. Instead, she recorded a video message urging world leaders to find solutions to the climate challenges facing our planet.*

I am delighted to welcome you all to the twenty-sixth United Nations Climate Change Conference; and it is perhaps fitting that you have come together in Glasgow, once a heartland of the industrial revolution, but now a place to address climate change.

This is a duty I am especially happy to discharge, as the impact of the environment on human progress was a subject close to the heart of my dear late husband, Prince Philip, The Duke of Edinburgh.

I remember well that in 1969, he told an academic gathering: 'If the world pollution situation is not critical at the moment, it is as certain as anything can be, that the situation will become increasingly intolerable within a very short time … If we fail to cope with this challenge, all the other problems will pale into insignificances.'

It is a source of great pride to me that the leading role my husband played in encouraging people to protect our fragile planet, lives on through the work of our eldest son Charles and his eldest son William. I could not be more proud of them. Indeed, I have drawn great comfort and inspiration from the relentless enthusiasm of people of all ages – especially the young – in calling for everyone to play their part.

In the coming days, the world has the chance to join in the shared objective of creating a safer, stabler future for our people and for the planet on which we depend. None of us underestimates the challenges ahead: but history has shown that when nations come together in common cause, there is always room for hope. Working side by side, we have the ability to solve the most insurmountable problems and to triumph over the greatest of adversities.

For more than seventy years, I have been lucky to meet and to know many of the world's great leaders. And I have perhaps come to understand a little about what made them special. It has sometimes been observed that what leaders do for their

people today is government and politics. But what they do for the people of tomorrow — that is statesmanship. I, for one, hope that this conference will be one of those rare occasions where everyone will have the chance to rise above the politics of the moment, and achieve true statesmanship.

It is the hope of many that the legacy of this summit – written in history books yet to be printed – will describe you as the leaders who did not pass up the opportunity, and that you answered the call of those future generations. That you left this conference as a community of nations with a determination, a desire, and a plan, to address the impact of climate change; and to recognise that the time for words has now moved to the time for action.

Of course, the benefits of such actions will not be there to enjoy for all of us here today: we none of us will live forever. But we are doing this not for ourselves but for our children and our children's children, and those who will follow in their footsteps. And so, I wish you every good fortune in this significant endeavour.

The Queen has long shared Sir David Attenborough's concerns about climate change. Here they chat at an event at Buckingham Palace in 2016, held to showcase forestry projects, part of a new conservation initiative named The Queen's Commonwealth Canopy.

# 2021

*The Queen paid tribute to her late husband Prince Philip in her Christmas Broadcast, which featured a series of photographs of their years together. She also looked forward to the celebrations of her Platinum Jubilee, to begin in February 2022.*

Although it's a time of great happiness and good cheer for many, Christmas can be hard for those who have lost loved ones. This year, especially, I understand why. But for me, in the months since the death of my beloved Philip, I have drawn great comfort from the warmth and affection of the many tributes to his life and work — from around the country, the Commonwealth and the world. His sense of service, intellectual curiosity and capacity to squeeze fun out of any situation — were all irrepressible. That mischievous, enquiring twinkle was as bright at the end as when I first set eyes on him.

But life, of course, consists of final partings as well as first meetings — and as much as I and my family miss him, I know he would want us to enjoy Christmas. We felt his presence as we, like millions around the world, readied ourselves for Christmas.

While COVID again means we can't celebrate quite as we may have wished, we can still enjoy the many happy traditions. Be it the singing of carols — as long as the tune is well known — decorating the tree, giving and receiving presents, or watching a favourite film where we already know the ending, it's no surprise that families so often treasure their Christmas routines. We see our own children and their families embrace the roles, traditions and values that mean so much to us, as these are passed from one generation to the next, sometimes being updated for changing times. I see it in my own family and it is a source of great happiness.

Prince Philip was always mindful of this sense of passing the baton. That's why he created The Duke of Edinburgh's Award, which offers young people throughout the Commonwealth and beyond the chance of exploration and adventure. It remains an astonishing success, grounded in his faith in the future.

He was also an early champion of taking seriously our stewardship of the environment, and I am proud beyond words that his pioneering work has been taken on and magnified by our eldest son Charles and his eldest son William — admirably supported by Camilla and Catherine — most recently at the COP climate change summit in Glasgow.

Next summer, we look forward to the Commonwealth Games. The baton is currently travelling the length and breadth of the Commonwealth, heading towards Birmingham, a beacon of hope on its journey. It will be a chance to celebrate the achievements of athletes and the coming-together of like-minded nations.

And February, just six weeks from now, will see the start of my Platinum Jubilee year, which I hope will be an opportunity for people everywhere to enjoy a sense of togetherness, a chance to give thanks for the enormous changes of the last 70 years — social, scientific and cultural — and also to look ahead with confidence.

I am sure someone somewhere today will remark that Christmas is a time for children. It's an engaging truth, but only half the story. Perhaps it's truer to say that Christmas can speak to the child within us all. Adults, when weighed down with worries, sometimes fail to see the joy in simple things, where children do not. And for me and my family, even with one familiar laugh missing this year, there will be joy in Christmas, as we have the chance to reminisce, and see anew the wonder of the festive season through the eyes of our young children, of whom we were delighted to welcome four more this year. They teach us all a lesson — just as the Christmas story does — that in the birth of a child, there is a new dawn with endless potential.

It is this simplicity of the Christmas story that makes it so universally appealing, simple happenings that formed the starting point of the life of Jesus — a man whose teachings have been handed down from generation to generation, and have been the bedrock of my faith. His birth marked a new beginning. As the carol says: 'The hopes and fears of all the years are met in thee tonight.' I wish you all a very happy Christmas.

The Queen waits alone at St George's Chapel, Windsor before the funeral of her 'beloved husband' Prince Philip, Duke of Edinburgh on 17 April, 2021. Because of coronavirus restrictions, only thirty guests attended the service, which was led by Justin Welby, Archbishop of Canterbury. The Duke died on 9 April, just a few months short of his 100th birthday.

# AFTERWORD:

When The Queen ascended the throne in 1952, the population of the UK was 50.6 million; today it stands at 68.2 million. Life expectancy was just over sixty-nine years; today it is eighty-one and rising. Our population then was largely white; today just over 11 per cent of our diverse country has its origins in Asia, Africa, and the Caribbean. When The Queen came to the throne, homosexuality was banned; now we welcome LGBTQ+ communities, and same-sex couples can be legally married across the UK. Rationing ended in 1954; in 2021 there were over 1,300 branches of McDonalds – but also increasing numbers of people reliant upon food banks. How we eat and what we eat and drink has been transformed. Even English wines win gold medals against their French counterparts.

During the seventy years of the Queen's reign, the UK has changed considerably – but the admiration for our reigning monarch has not wavered; her expertise in fulfilling her role having consistently impressed not only the general public but also leaders and public figures around the world.

During a joint press conference with former Prime Minister David Cameron in 2016, President Obama even made a heartfelt confession about her, saying of Her Majesty: 'She is truly one of my favourite people.' Nelson Mandela was also a huge fan of the Queen, always addressing her off-camera as 'My dear friend Elizabeth', and that reverence was reflected on-camera, too, as shown during the speech he gave whilst on an official visit to the UK in July 1996: 'It is indeed an honour to be received by Her Majesty this evening, an honour for our government; for the South African nation, and for me personally.'

Sir Winston Churchill and the Queen had a close personal relationship. During his time as an MP (from 1900 to 1922 and then again from 1924 to 1964), he represented five different constituencies, first as a Conservative then as a Liberal and finally as a Conservative, and served as PM twice; from 1940–45 and 1951–55. At his funeral in 1965, The Queen broke protocol by arriving at St Paul's Cathedral ahead of his family. Churchill's enormous admiration for Elizabeth was evident from the day of her coronation, as was abundantly clear in his prime ministerial broadcast to the nation that very evening: 'Here at the summit of our worldwide community is a lady whom we respect because she is our Queen and whom we love because she is herself.' Such reverence towards our reigning monarch is widely seen today, Churchill's pronouncement on her coronation day ringing as true now as it did seventy years ago.

God bless you, Ma'am.

In his role as Colonel of the Grenadier Guards, Prince Philip was standing ready
to escort The Queen for a review of the Grenadier Guards' elite Queen's
Regiment at Windsor Castle in 2003, when a swarm of bees descended. The
sight of guests running for cover gave The Queen a most uncharacteristic,
but rather lovely, public fit of the giggles.

# SPEECH FINDER
## *At a Glance*

## 1992 – 2001

### Into the New Millennium

## 2002 – 2011

### Heirs to the Throne

## 2012 – 2021

### The Diamond Years

At-a-glance guide to all Her Majesty's Christmas Broadcasts from 1952 to 2021 inclusive, and all the Feature Speeches chosen for this celebratory book. You can find many more of The Queen's inspiring speeches, from throughout her reign, at www.royal.uk.

Published in hardback in Great Britain in 2022 by Allen & Unwin, an imprint of Atlantic Books Ltd.

Foreword by Jennie Bond
Additional text by Derek Wyatt

10 9 8 7 6 5 4 3 2 1

A CIP catalogue record for this book is available from the British Library.

Produced and designed by Elwin Street Agency Ltd.
10 Elwin Street
London E2 7BU
United Kingdom

Designer: Moira Clinch
Editor: Sarah Kilby

All pictures supplied by Getty, except the following:
Page 6, 168: Alamy
Page 62: Mary Evans
Page 225, 243: Shutterstock
Page 249: London Olympics/Youtube

Allen & Unwin
An imprint of Atlantic Books Ltd
Ormond House
26–27 Boswell Street
London
WC1N 3JZ

www.allenandunwin.com/uk

Hardback ISBN: 978 1 83895 672 1

Printed in Great Britain by Bell and Bain Ltd, Glasgow